PINSTRII
AND VEHICLE GRAPHICS

BY JOHN HANNUKAINE

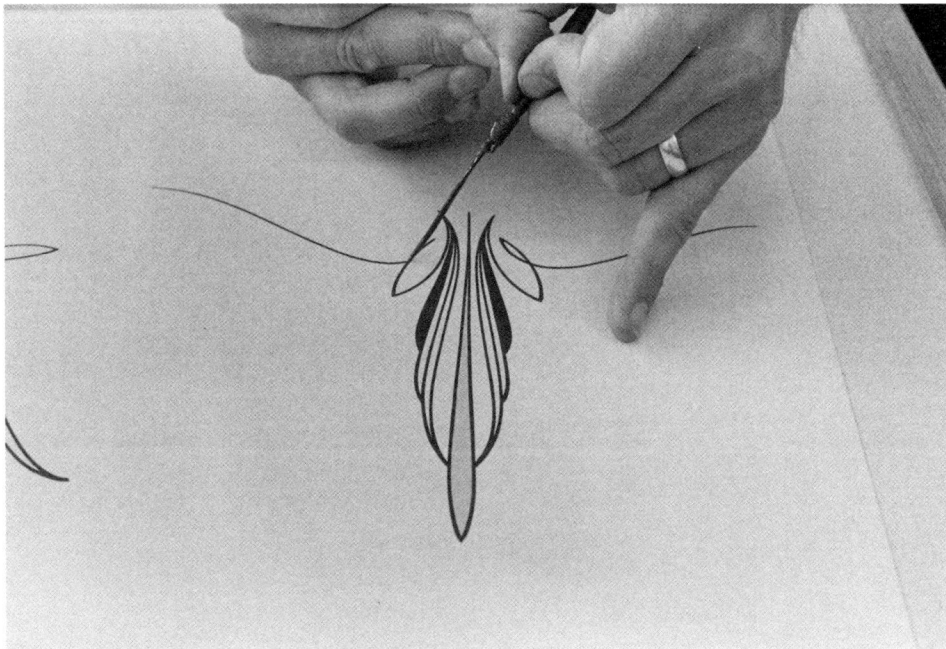

A STEP-BY-STEP GUIDE TO HAND-APPLIED VEHICLE GRAPHICS

TABLE OF CONTENTS

ABOUT THE AUTHOR

John F. "Butch" Hannukaine has been pinstriping and painting signs since he was 15. Born in 1945, John became interested in pinstriping during a family vacation to northern California, where he began noticing the thin line designs on hot rods and motorcycles. He bought a striping brush and some lettering enamel, and began striping anything he could. The very first thing he pinstriped was a shovel.

After about two years of pinstriping as a hobby, John began to realize he could market his developing striping skills. In addition to the lines and designs he added to vehicles, John found that people were also interested in cartoons and lettering — which eventually led him into the sign business.

John says he "lettered his way through college," working freelance and with several Seattle-area shops. He graduated from the University of Washington with a degree in art education, then joined the Navy and spent two years working as an illustrator draftsman.

He left the Navy, opened his own sign shop, and eight years later had eight employees and a 5000-square-foot shop. The hectic pace began to grow tiresome, though, so John closed the shop and found a quiet place in the shadow of Mt. Rainier where he could pinstripe vehicles and make signs. His current shop is the 1500-square-foot barn behind his home. Working at home affords him time to spend with his wife, Bonnie, and their three children, Rachel, Adam, and Alison.

Pinstriping and vehicle graphics

make up a large part of John's shop volume. But don't think that you'll have to visit the Olympia, Washington, area to see any of John's work first-hand — for much of the summer, you can find John and Bonnie pinstriping at various motorcycle rallies across the West. Since he began working the rally circuit some five years ago, John's work has become very popular.

When he's not striping or making signs, John is often fishing for steelhead or salmon in the many streams around his home in Tumwater, Washington. Other "spare time" pursuits include waterfowl carving, water and oil painting (John is an award-winning fine artist), taxidermy, and music.

John with silver salmon

Some of John's watercolor work

INTRODUCTION

I can't count the times I've been striping in public and heard someone say, "Gee, I wish I could do that," or, "I could never do anything like that — I wouldn't even know where to start!"

Boy, do I know that feeling! While I was attending college (about 20 years ago) I really wanted to learn to do gold leaf window work. I read everything on the subject that I could find, and tried many times — without much success — to gild on glass. Then one day I came across a book called *Gold Leaf Techniques*, by Raymond J. LeBlanc. This book was well written and had lots of photos and easy-to-understand step-by-step procedures. After reading the first four chapters I went out and did a gold job on an optometrist's window, and it came out very well.

Since then I've always thought that if I had the opportunity to share in the way Mr. LeBlanc did, I would. That's why I wrote this book. For me, learning and sharing what you have learned is a big part of what life is all about.

The goal of this book is to explain and demonstrate pinstriping in a simple form so that even someone with little or no experience could, with some study and practice, produce satisfying work in a relatively short period of time. I also hope to pass along some of the more advanced techniques which are becoming so popular today.

There is no "right" or "wrong" pinstriping — that's really just a matter of taste and personal preference. Some people like the subtle, conservative work of stripers like Mitch Kim of Portland,

FOR ME, SHARING WHAT YOU HAVE LEARNED IS A BIG PART OF WHAT LIFE IS ALL ABOUT

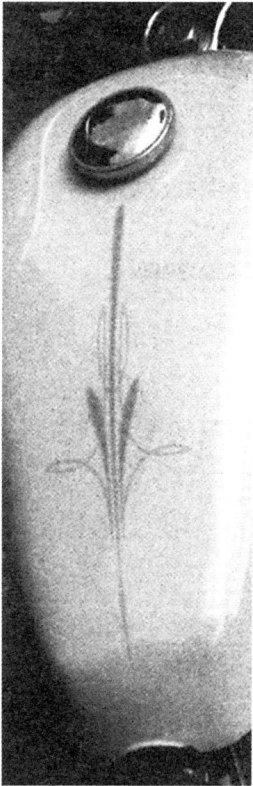

Oregon. Others prefer colorful, flamboyant styles like that of Steve Kafka of Phoenix, Arizona. I like it all!

But while there is no "right" or "wrong" pinstriping, I *do* believe there is proper and improper technique. In this book, I have tried to show the proper tools, materials, and procedures that will allow you to produce technically correct jobs regardless of the style you end up doing.

Pinstriping has seen many changes in the past five years, and I'm sure it will continue to grow and evolve. Part of this book is devoted to demonstrating some of the new hand-applied graphic techniques used by myself and many other stripers around the country. All the work done in this book was done with lettering enamels and hand-applied (with the exception of some of the airbrushed projects).

I believe the gallery section is an important part of this book. It gave me the opportunity to show some of the excellent and varied work of a few of the country's best pinstripers. It gives a well-rounded view of just what striping and graphics can be. I'd like to thank these artists for sharing their work, and all those artists and friends who have shared unselfishly with me during the past 30 years of my career. I also want to thank my loving and supportive family, and most of all, the good Lord for giving me the gift of being interested in artistic things.

I hope you learn from this book. Don't be afraid to stretch yourself and try something different. Good luck and enjoy yourself.

John Hannukaine
Tumwater, Washington
September, 1991

CHAPTER ONE: TOOLS

When doing any kind of project, it helps if you have everything that you need right at your fingertips. I've found that a TV tray works great for this, especially when it comes to pinstriping projects. They're lightweight, collapsible, easy to move around, and will stand on uneven surfaces.

I also recommend that you invest in an inexpensive office chair — the kind with wheels, hydraulic height adjustment, and a comfortable padded seat. Remove the back, and you're set. A seat like this will allow you to work comfortably at different heights all day, and will probably increase your productivity.

Now back to the tray. Here's what I keep on it:

✗ Denatured alcohol in a plastic atomizer (spray bottle) for cleaning up smudges and goofs

✗ Paper towels — great for clean-up because they don't leave any lint

✗ A discarded magazine to be used as

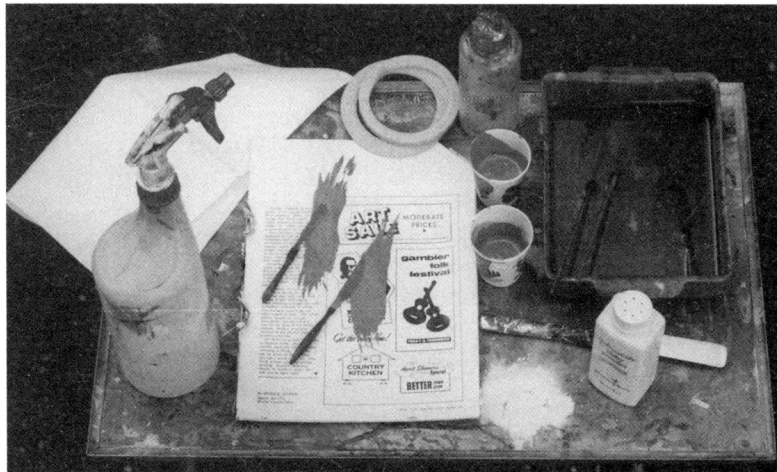

a palette

✗ A few rolls of tape — fine line tape and masking tape

✗ "1 Shot"® Reducer No. 6000 in a squirt bottle

✗ Paint, mixed-to-match in un-waxed paper bathroom cups, thinned with reducer. I usually add a drop or two of Smoothie or similar fish-eye eliminator, too.

✗ A shallow pan with some thinner in it. I lay my brushes in it when I'm not using them.

✗ My trusty palette knife! I use it for cutting paint skins off cans and cups, for taking paint out of the can, and for mixing.

✗ Baby powder — this allows the fingers of my striping hand to glide smoothly across the vehicle's surface.

Paints, thinners, and additives

Over the years I have used a variety of different brands of enamel paint for lettering and striping. Of all that I have tried, I have found "1 Shot" Lettering Enamel (Consumers Paint Factory, Inc., 5300 W. 5th Ave., Gary, IN 46406) works best for me. Nearly all of their colors are very opaque, and when thinned with "1 Shot" reducers, they dry to a hard, glossy finish.

The "1 Shot" reducer I most frequently use is Reducer No. 6000. Along with a drop or two of Smoothie or similar product (mixed into about ½ inch of paint in the bottom of a small paper

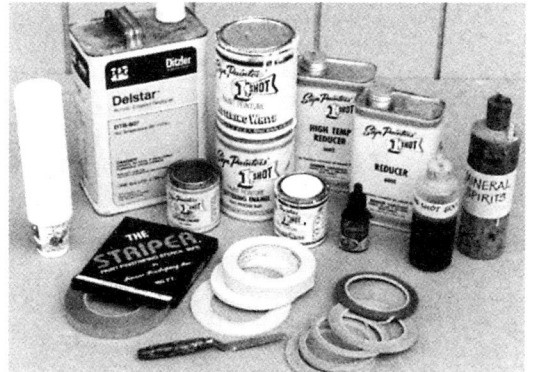

cup), this reducer thins the paint to the proper consistency and still allows it to dry properly. If it's really hot out, I'll use High Temp Reducer 6002 instead.

On occasion, I have thinned my paint with Ditzler Delstar Acrylic Enamel Reducer DTR-607 (PPG Industries, Inc., Ditzler Automotive Finishes, Troy, MI 48084). It helps the paint flow out nicely and dry to a hard finish. The only disadvantage is the unpleasant odor.

I put my reducer and mineral spirits in plastic squirt bottles. It's easier to get the exact amount I want in exactly the right place this way.

I keep a low-sided pan filled with mineral spirits nearby while striping. I lay the brushes I'm not using in it. If I happen to need a little extra thinning, I can dip the brush in the pan rather than squirt some out of the bottle.

Tape

I use ⅛" and ¼" masking tape to lay out straight line work. Then I stripe as close as possible to the tape without actually touching it with the brush. (Sometimes I'll use the tape as a guide under my middle finger.) If the brush touches the tape, complete the stripe and remove the tape. Then go back with a little denatured alcohol on a rag, wipe off the flaw, and touch it up.

I use ¾" masking tape for some of my layout work and general masking. *Don't use cheap tape*, since it is likely to leave some adhesive on the surface. I use 3M tape and have found that it always works well.

I use Scotch Fine Line No. 218 tape (made by 3M) for masking lettering, graphics, and stripes that I want to fill in with my brush. This tape adheres tightly to the surface, and doesn't allow paint to leak in underneath it.

If you need extreme flexibility when laying out graphics, try Scotch Plastic Tape No. 471 in ⅛" or ¼" widths. It's blue (which makes it easy to see) and adheres tightly to the surface.

WHEN
STRIPING, IT
IS ESSENTIAL
TO WORK
ON A CLEAN
SURFACE

I'll sometimes use Finesse striping tape (Finesse Pinstriping, Inc., P.O. Box 541428, Linden Hill Station, Flushing, NY 11354) for some of my graphics work (see the blend step-by-step in Chapter 5). It is a fill-in-type tape. You apply it, peel off the backing, then paint down the exposed stripes. When you're done you peel off the tape itself, and you're left with a single line or multiple parallel lines. It is available in many sizes and line configurations.

Surface prep

When pinstriping, lettering, or doing any other form of graphic arts work on vehicles, it is essential to work on a clean surface. A clean surface is free from wax, grease, silicone, poly sealants, and static electricity. If lettering enamel, or any paint or film for that matter, is applied to an unclean surface, adhesion problems are likely.

I have used a variety of cleaning products over the years, and am now using the products shown in the photo.

For general pre-paint clean-up, for instance, on a custom car or new repaint job, I use Acryli-Clean DX 330 Wax and Grease Remover (PPG Industries, Inc., Strongsville, OH, 44136; 440-572-2800). I apply the solvent with a clean paper towel and wipe it off with another.

If I'm working on plastic car or motorcycle parts, all this rubbing will have generated an amazing amount of static electricity. The surface becomes so

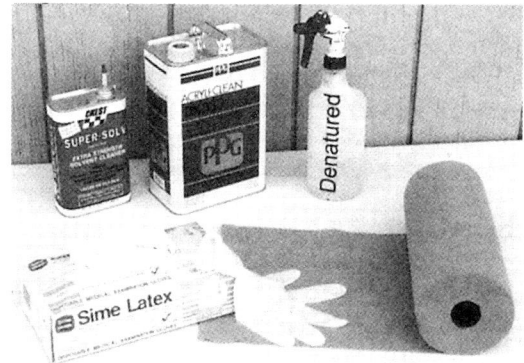

charged that it will pull the paint right out of the brush before it touches the surface. In this case I spray the surface with denatured alcohol and wipe it with a clean paper towel. Keep the wiping to a minimum, or you'll recharge the surface.

When working on new cars, where I feel a stronger solvent is required, I now use a product called Super-Solv (Crest Industries, Inc., Wyandotte, MI, 48192; 313-283-4100). I apply and remove it the same as Acryli-Clean, except that I go through the process twice. It does a great job of cleaning off the sealants that manufacturers and dealers apply.

Remember to wear rubber gloves when handling these products and follow all the safety precautions on the containers.

Brushes

Different brushes have different uses. I use three types of brushes—sword stripers, outliners, and quills—for almost all my striping and graphics work. In the photo below I've laid out all the brushes I use most frequently in my day-to-day striping jobs. Starting from the left, here's how I like to use them:

The first brush is an Xcaliber, which is designed and sold by Mr. J (276 Green Ave., Lyndhurst, NJ, 07071; 201-935-4510). The brush has shorter hair than

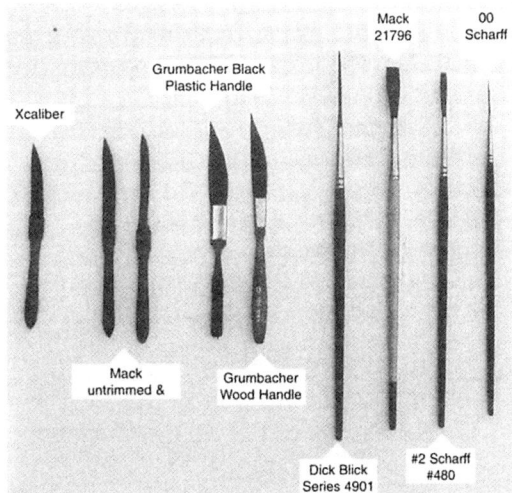

Xcaliber

Grumbacher Black Plastic Handle

Mack 21796

00 Scharff

Mack untrimmed &

Grumbacher Wood Handle

Dick Blick Series 4901

#2 Scharff #480

most other striping brushes. I use it for my old-style symmetrical designs.

The next two brushes are the original Mack striping brush, untrimmed and trimmed. It is a good brush for most pinstriping designs and a pretty fair straight liner, too. When it is moderately trimmed it becomes very flexible, and when radically trimmed it becomes nearly as "snakey" as an outliner. These brushes are available from Andrew Mack & Sons Brush Co. (P.O. Box 157, Jonesville, MI, 49250; 517-849-9272).

The metal ferrule striping brushes in the middle are both Grumbacher brushes that I get from Sid Moses (Seelig Custom, 10456 Santa Monica Blvd., Los Angeles, CA, 90025; 310-475-1111). These brushes, in the 1, 0, and 00 sizes, are my first choice for straight line work.

The next brush is an Eclipse Outliner, Series 4901, by Dick Blick (Galesburg, IL, 61401; 800-634-7001). I use this brush in a No. 3 size for most of my scroll designs and wild script lettering.

The third brush from the right is a metal ferruled lettering brush made by Mack. I prefer to use them for fill-in, lettering, and cartoons. They hold their shape well and don't lose hairs.

The last two brushes are Scharff #480 "Syn-Sable" scroller brushes. I get them at the local art store and use them for fine lettering and detail work.

All of these brushes have been soaked in neatsfoot oil, groomed, and placed as they would be between jobs. It's important to store them with the hairs groomed straight and laid flat. If a brush gets kinked, though, it can be straightened. Wash it thoroughly with warm water and soap, groom the hairs straight, then set aside to dry. Once it is dry, oil and store it properly.

Brush care

Before I use a brush, I rinse the oil out with thinner. After each use during the work day, I rinse it again with thinner and lay it in a shallow tray that contains about a half-inch of thinner. I rest the handles on the edge of the tray, and the brush is ready for the next use.

When I'm finished painting for the day, I rinse my brushes in the pan of thinner they have been in all day. I remove the brush from the thinner and wipe it with a rag to eliminate as much paint and dirty thinner as I can. Next I rinse the brush again, this time in clean thinner.

I then dip the brush in neatsfoot oil and make sure the oil gets through all the hairs and into the heel. Before putting the brush away, I stroke and shape it with my fingers.

Step-by-step: Trimming a brush

The series of photos on the following pages show how I trim a brush.

Why do I trim a striping brush? Because it makes it easier to use and produces a cleaner line. The short hairs on the underside of an untrimmed brush tend to flip out straight while executing tight, circular strokes. This causes ragged lines. A properly trimmed brush becomes very flexible and turns sharp corners better, while requiring very little rolling.

I soak these brushes in neatsfoot oil and use them for general striping and fill-in for two or three months before I select and trim them. That's about how long it takes for them to soften up, and to reach a point where you can see the true character of the brush.

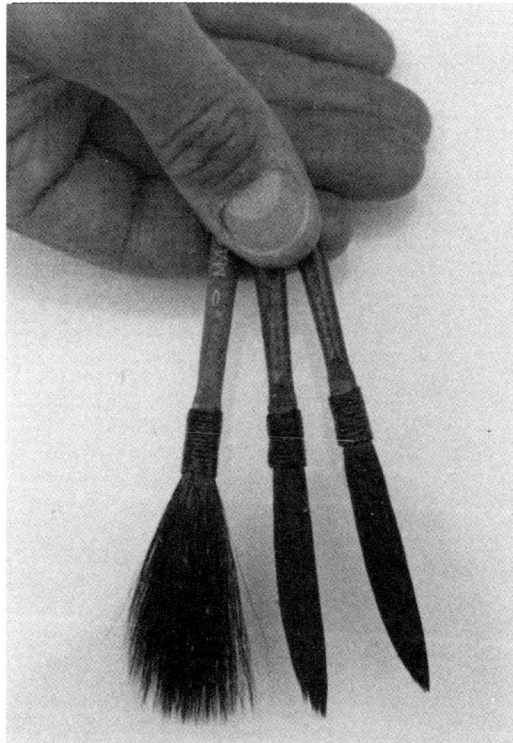

Figure 1. The brush on the left in this photo is a Mack sword striper as you would get it from the store — fluffy and dry.

The middle brush is a Mack 00 which has been soaked in neatsfoot oil and groomed. Because of its ragged end, I would not select this brush to trim for fine line or scroll work. It would be acceptable for general medium-weight line work and filling in, though.

The right-hand brush is also a groomed and oiled Mack 00. Because the tip is nice and smooth, this is the brush we'll trim.

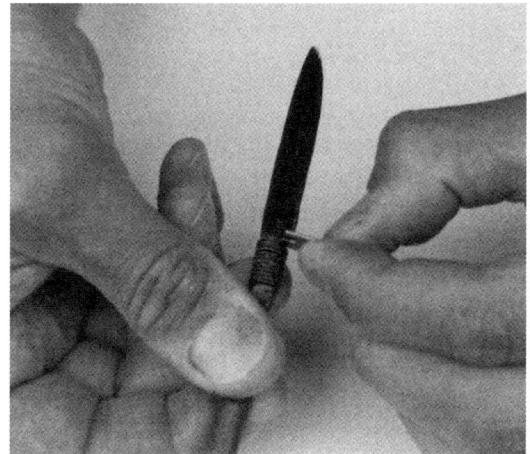

Figure 2. Using a single-edged razor blade, I trim about an ⅛" of hair from the bottom, or short side, of the brush. That's because as you pull the sword around in circles, it's the short hairs on the bottom of the brush that get in the way. I trim my brushes to different degrees for different applications — I use a less radically trimmed brush for less swirly work, a more radically trimmed brush for tighter work. The sides of the brush usually don't require trimming.

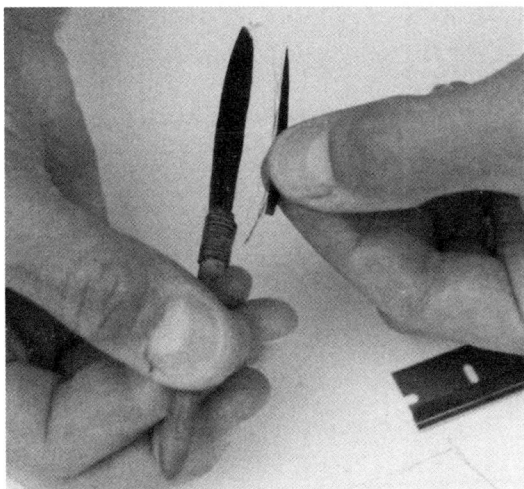

Figure 3. This photo shows me holding what I trimmed in the previous photo. Next I'll trim a small amount from the top of the brush, along with any stragglers at the tip of the brush.

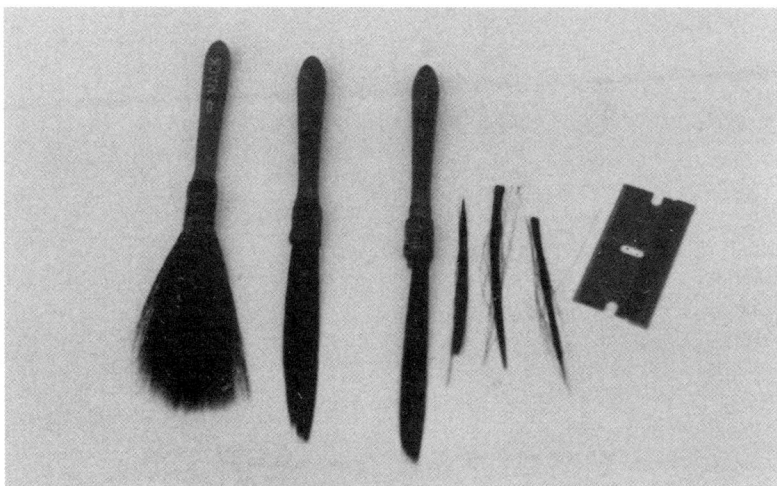

Figure 4. Here's the new brush, the untrimmed oiled brush, the trimmed oiled brush, the trimmings, and a single-edged razor blade. This trimmed brush was used to do the examples shown in Chapter Three of this book.

CHAPTER TWO: LONG LINES

Long line pinstriping is used to highlight a vehicle's curves and body shape. It can make a vehicle look longer or lower, depending on where it is placed. In most cases, it will run the length of a vehicle's body, or along the contours of a body panel. A long stripe that is run parallel to an adjacent molding is great for pinstripers, because the molding gives us something to anchor our fingers to and use as a point of reference.

I don't think there is anything much better-looking than a perfectly executed double-line stripe job down the side of a hot rod, custom car, or new car. It adds an extra element that enhances the appearance of the vehicle. I especially like the double-line jobs that are done in two colors — colors that blend in with the color of the vehicle. And if the stripes are very thin, so much the better.

There are three factors which should remain constant in order to produce a long, straight line of constant weight. They are paint consistency, pressure and angle of the brush, and speed.

Paint consistency is very important. If it's too thin, the paint will spread and the brush won't track right. The paint is too thick if it skips, makes blobs, and will not go as far as it should. When the paint is just right, the brush will track properly and leave a stripe three to four feet in length — sometimes as long as six feet.

The second factor, pressure and angle of the brush, is determined by your grip on the brush. The photograph on the following page (Figure 5) illustrates the proper grip for long line striping. The

LONG LINE STRIPING CAN MAKE A VEHICLE APPEAR LONGER OR LOWER

LEARNING
TO STRIPE
IS A LOT LIKE
LEARNING TO
PLAY A
MUSICAL
INSTRUMENT

only time I modify this grip is when I lock my little, ring, and middle fingers over a molding.

The last factor is speed, which is controlled by the rate at which you move and pull your arm while striping. Load the brush so that you can pull the longest line possible without lifting the

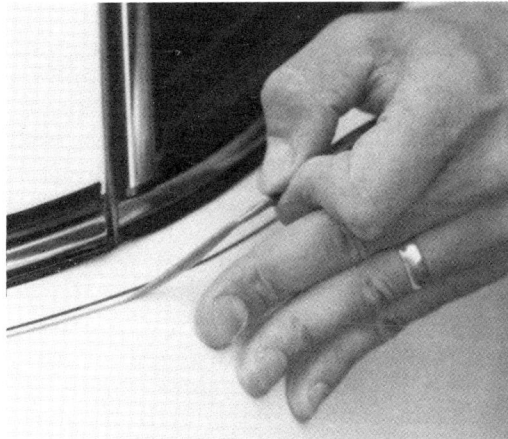

Figure 5

brush. This often means walking backward while pulling the brush. Treat your brush hand as if it were a machine that you pull with the rest of your body.

A note about practicing

If you want to improve your pinstriping and vehicle graphics skills, it is absolutely essential that you practice — especially when you're just starting out. Handling a brush, whether it is a lettering brush or a striping brush, requires muscle dexterity and eye-to-hand coordination that can only be learned by practicing and experimenting. Learning to stripe or letter is a lot like learning to play a musical instrument.

Find a smooth surface to practice on. I like using acrylic sheeting or painted hardboard. For practicing really wild techniques, those materials work better than a new Jaguar or Infiniti. When you get some work you're happy with, use these panels for sales examples. Keep these practice panels and go back to look at them from time to time — they can help you see the progress you've made.

As you progress, you'll probably start doing most of your experimenting right on the job. Remember — if you don't like something you've painted, just wipe it off and try something different.

Points to remember

Brush selection is very important. I use untrimmed Germany brushes in 0 and 00 sizes for most of my long-line work. The weight of the line can be varied by working off different portions of the brush. But like a lettering quill, a striping sword has a comfortable area at which it performs best. That's why it's probably best to switch between different size brushes, depending on the line weight you're looking for. It's just not smart to use a No. 1 to do 00 work — it can be done, but it's not smart.

When pulling a long line on a vehicle, don't be distracted by mirrors, moldings, or door handles — keep your

brush hand locked in position and let it ride over all those obstacles like a track on a tank. The important thing is that you support the brush with the same pressure constantly.

Paletting

It doesn't matter whether you're oil painting, sign painting, or pinstriping, a brush has to be paletted. Paletting loads

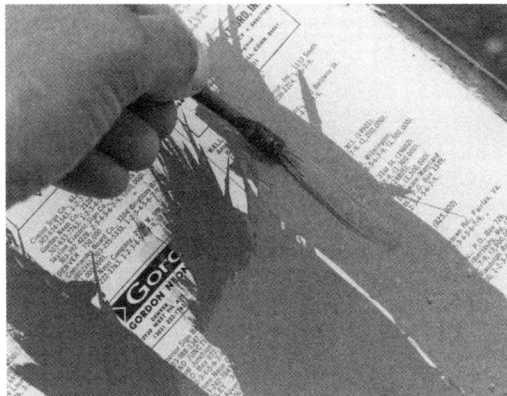

Figure 6

WHEN PULL-
ING A LONG
LINE ON A
VEHICLE,
DON'T BE
DISTRACTED
BY MIRRORS,
MOLDINGS,
OR DOOR
HANDLES

the brush with paint, straightens out all the hairs, and allows you to work the paint to the proper consistency (Figure 6).

Practice will teach you this very quickly: if the paint has too much thinner in it, it will be watery and feel slippery on the palette. If you try to stripe with this paint, your brush will not track straight. But if the paint is too thick, it will feel sticky as you palette the brush. If you try to stripe with thick paint, the brush will only travel a short distance and will leave a broken, uneven line.

When paint has the right amount of reducer in it, it will palette freely with a nice, smooth pull to it. If the paint feels too thick as you palette, dip the tip of the brush into the thinner in the brush pan. Work this into your brush by stroking it back and forth on the palette. If it's too thin, add more paint.

Striping with paint that is of the proper consistency allows the brush to track properly and produce smooth, even lines without spreading, running, or skipping.

Using a molding as a guide

Let's start off by looking at a basic long line striping job. In this first example, we'll run a double line along a molding.

An example of John's work

For the sake of photographing this demonstration, we did it outdoors. But I prefer to do my striping inside where there's no wind — wind tends to blow the brush around and prematurely dry the paint. Working inside the shop also gives me greater control over lighting and temperature.

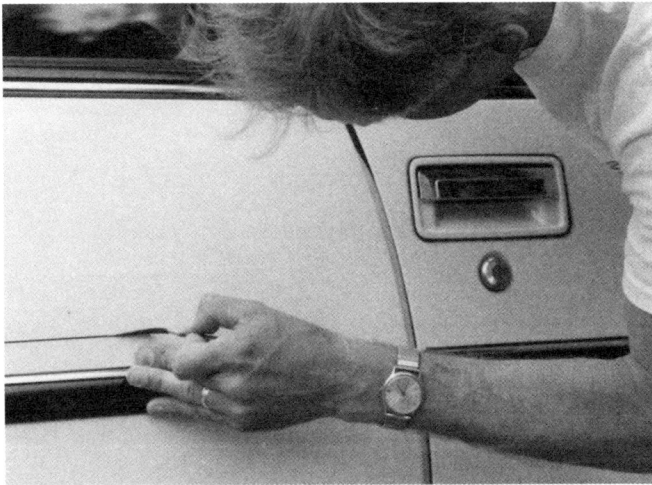

Figure 7. Once your hand is locked in position and you can see that the pressure on the brush is such that it is producing a line of the desired weight, all that's left to do is pull the line.

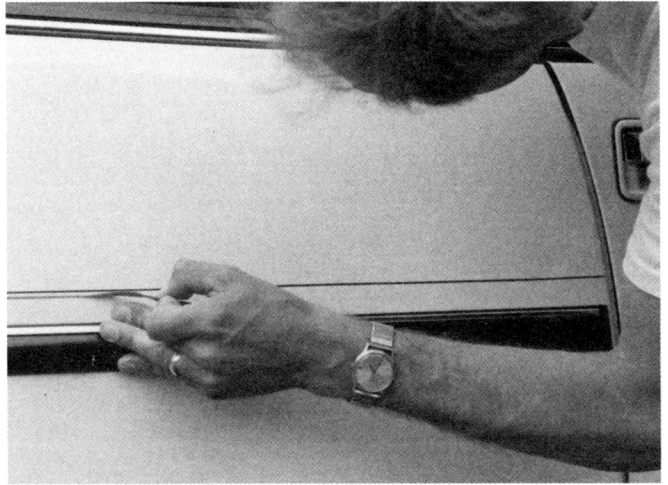

Figure 8. This photo shows me adding a second stripe in a different color. Hand position remains the same; just mind the second line and make it uniform in weight and parallel to the first. This takes a lot of concentration.

Using tape as a guide

Fine masking tape is often used by stripers to provide a visual guide for the striping. The theory is simple — lay down the masking tape and make sure it's straight (even if you have to reposition it a time or two). Once it's in position, you can use the tape as a guide and stripe beside it.

Taping is a visual thing — it may take me an hour to get all the lines and panels taped off on a really involved project. For a simple double line like the one shown here, though, taping only takes a few minutes.

I usually use ⅛" masking tape for taping off long lines. Quarter inch tape works, too, but the ⅛" tape really likes going around corners.

Long line striping is multi-faceted; I mind the angle, pressure, and speed of the brush, while at the same time keeping an eye on the line's proximity to the lettering tape, molding, or adjacent line. Once you lock your hand in position and begin pulling a line, the rest comes naturally (with practice, of course!).

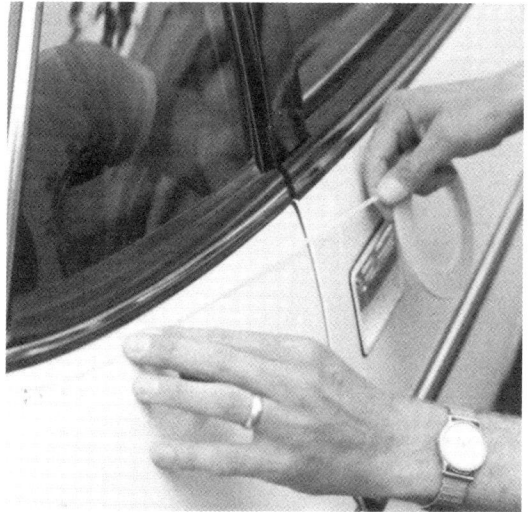

Figure 9. Apply the tape by pulling it off the roll with one hand, while pressing it into position with the other. Since I'm left-handed, I usually hold the tape in my right hand and adhere it with my left.

Figure 10. Carefully examine the placement of the tape before you wet a brush; it's easier to move the line now than later. Once the tape is in place, I just get my brush and paint cup, and start striping. I've found that working right out of the cup is more efficient than going back and forth to the palette. Paint stays fresher in the cup and saves a lot of walking back and forth to your palette.

Figure 11. You may find that while pulling — or trying to pull — a long line on a vehicle, the fingers on your brush hand may stick to the surface. I keep a bottle of baby powder on my stand and use it when I'm doing long line work. I daub the fingers of my lettering hand that are going to ride on the surface of the vehicle in it, and that allows my hand to glide along more smoothly.

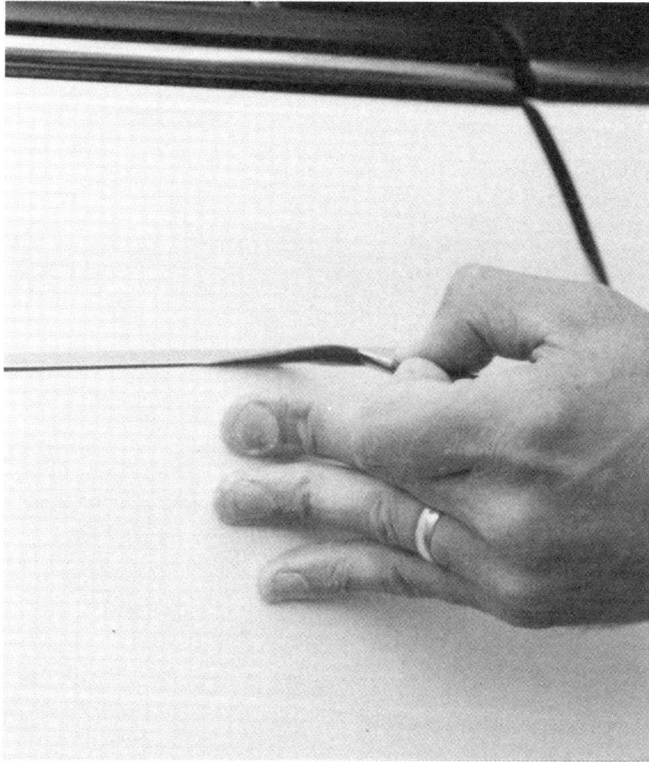

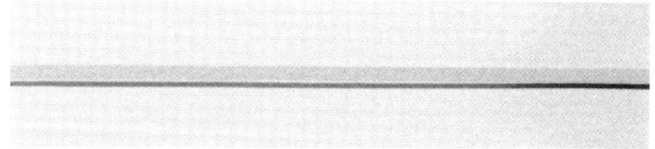

Figure 13. The fine line between the tape and line is evident in this photo.

Figure 12. This photo illustrates proper hand position and the space between the stripe and the tape. It's important to remember that when pulling a line next to tape, use the tape only as a point of reference. When done properly, there is a gap of about 1/64" left between the edge of the stripe and the edge of the tape. If the paint touches the tape, there will be a bleed-out mark on the edge of the stripe when the tape is removed.

Figure 14. When the first line is finished, remove the tape. The first line will now serve as a guide for the placement of the second line.

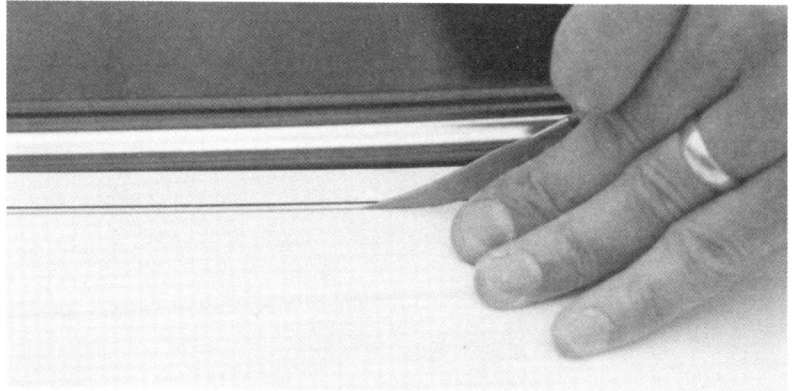

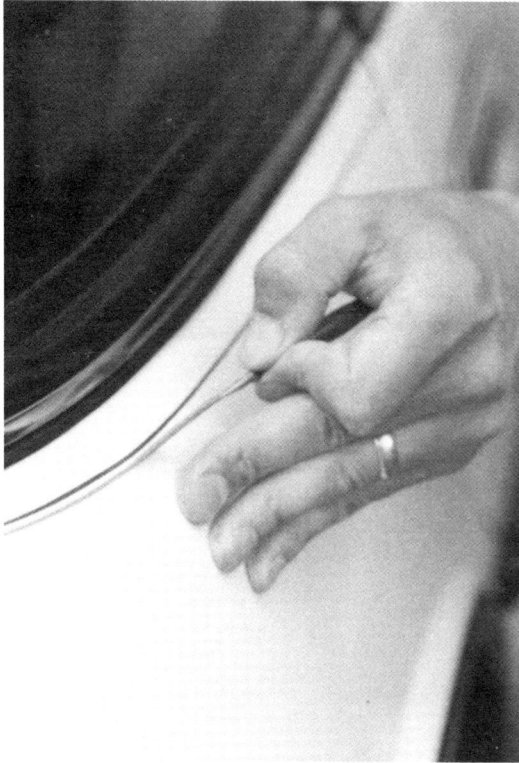

Figure 16

Figures 15, 16, 17. Use the same hand position that you used for the first line. Guide off the first line, and repeat the process. When continuing å stroke, put the brush down a few inches into the stroke you are continuing.

Figure 17

Figure 18. This shows that the hand position essentially remains the same through the turn.

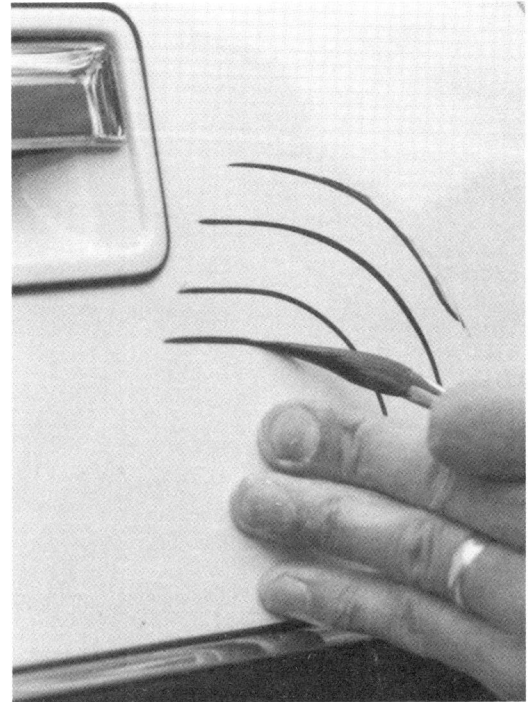

Figure 19. You can see how ragged the top arc in this series is. That raggedness is caused by the short hairs on the bottom of the brush. The only way around that is to gently roll the bottom of the brush into the inside of the curve; this gets them up out of the way, and allows you to make the line with the long hairs that make up the top of the brush. Another option is to roll the brush slightly before you begin the stroke.

There are times in fine line striping when you may want to turn a line a full 90 degrees or better. Straight line brushes, because of their construction, aren't adept at such things — so it takes some maneuvering to coax a straight line brush through a sharp curve.

The maneuver itself is ever so subtle — it's a gentle roll of the sword. This is one of the few moves that calls for me to roll my brush; and the roll is so subtle that it is barely perceptible in a photograph.

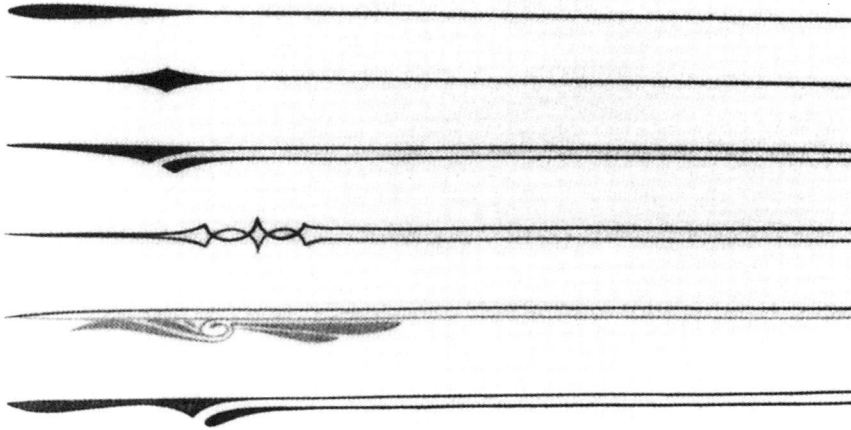

Figure 20. When I get to the end of a single or double line, I always add some kind of finishing touch. Here are six ideas I have used, but the possibilities are endless.

CHAPTER THREE: BASIC DESIGNS

Most of the traditional pinstriping that we see on motorcycles, 18-wheelers, and cars is simply a collage of reasonably simple brush maneuvers. This type of striping evolved from the "coach striping" of years ago, and experienced a popularity explosion during the 1950s and '60s. Since then it has ebbed and flowed in popularity, and has evolved through the work of a number of great pinstripers.

By studying my own work, and the work of other stripers who I look to for inspiration, I have isolated six basic "moves" which can be connected and altered to form effective pinstriping designs. The possibilities really are endless; as I said in the introduction, there is no "right" or "wrong" style of striping.

Using your fingers as a palette

Whether I am lettering or striping, I always try to keep my hands as clean as possible. When hands get covered with paint, they get sticky — this is uncomfortable and affects dexterity.

But more importantly, the paint we use for pinstriping has lead in it. That's

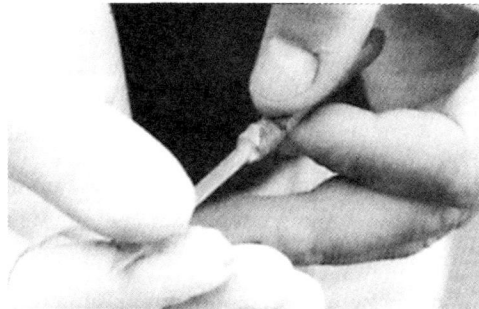

Wear gloves when handling paint

MOST OF MY DESIGNS EVOLVE AS THEY GO TOGETHER

why it covers so well. But lead is potentially harmful, as are many of the other chemicals found in paint.

I usually palette my brush on a

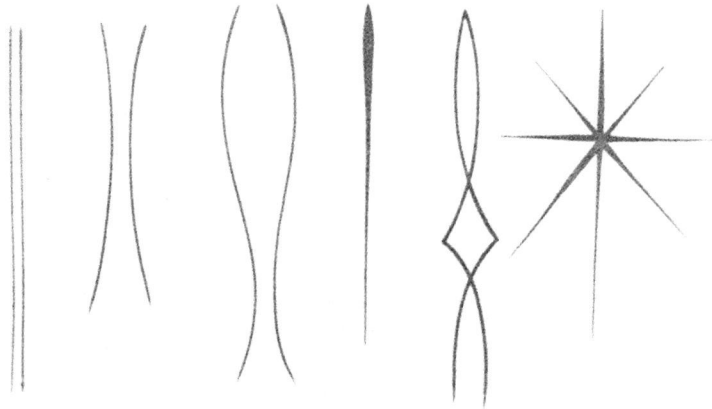

Figure 21. Here are the six shapes we want to learn to lead our brush through: the straight line, the single curve, the reverse curve, the thick-and-thin, the crossover, and the star. The crossover is constructed from two overlapping single curves, and the star is made up of four thick-and-thins.

magazine or the inside edge of the paper cup I'm working out of. But when I'm striping designs (such as those found in the section on basic designs), I like to use my fingers as a palette. After laying down a stroke on the work surface, I stroke the brush lightly between my thumb and forefinger and pull the paint from the heel to the tip and groom the tip.

Because of the apparent health risks, I have started wearing a disposable examination glove on my palette hand. Not only does it keep the paint off my fingers while paletting — it also eliminates the need to clean my palette hand with harsh solvents. These gloves are inexpensive, and available from most paint supply stores.

The six basic maneuvers

Let's take a look at these six basic maneuvers (photo at left) and see how they can be used.

In this series of photos (Figures 22-

33), I'm using a moderately trimmed Mack striper in size 0. Since we're working on mastering the basics, we'll stick to one color of paint thinned to the proper consistency. You'll want to palette the brush first on one side, then on the other, as many times as it takes to get a good feel (a nice, smooth drag).

Figure 22. In order to pull a line that is straight and uniform in width, three things must remain constant: pressure, brush angle, and speed. I achieve this by anchoring my hands as shown in this photo. Granted, there are times when I must lift one or both fingers from the work surface in order to avoid smearing wet paint, but this approach to holding the brush guarantees that pressure and brush angle will remain constant. Speed is the only variable left once the brush is anchored in your hands. That is executed by pulling toward you the "machine" that your hands and brush have become.

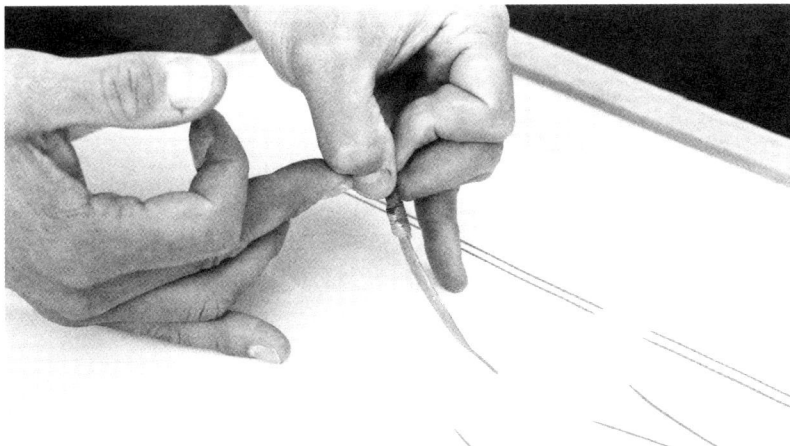

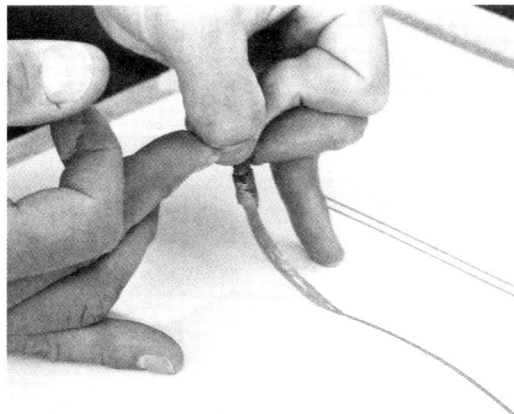

Figure 24

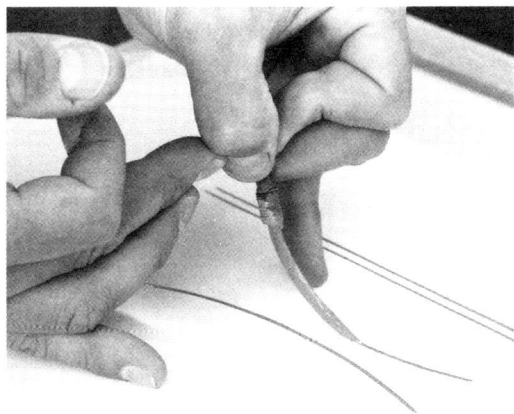

Figure 25

Figures 23, 24, and 25. Once you've made a few series of straight lines, move on to the single curve. Hand position remains the same. Avoid the temptation to anchor your little fingers on the surface and execute the curve with your fingers that are holding the brush — your brush and hands should move together as a unit. There is a measure of body movement that takes place as you stripe. It varies with the striper and the situation — sometimes you may only be able to move your arms, and other times you may find that you're gently moving your whole body with the stroke.

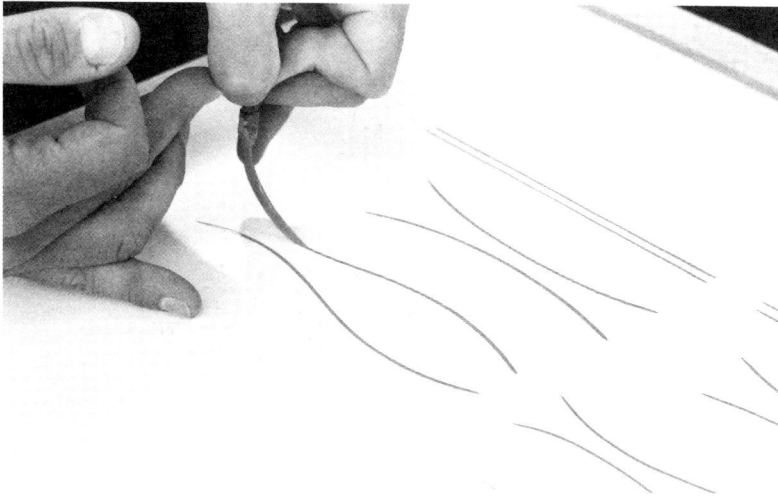

Figure 26. The reverse curve is executed similar to the single curve, only the line continues around to form an "S" shape. You can see in this photo that as I approach the end of the stroke, I use the thumb and forefinger which are holding the brush to pull it toward me, which naturally changes the angle of the brush. Just remember to maintain the weight of the line — it must remain constant.

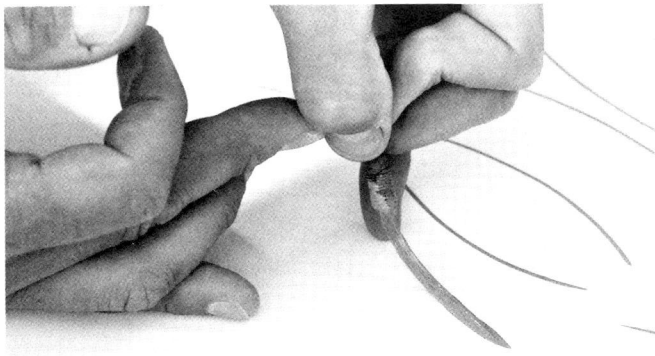

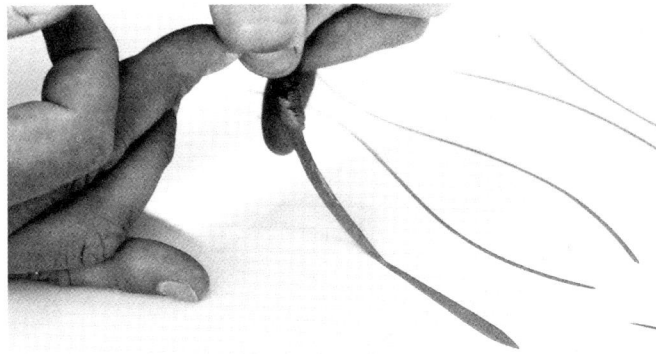

Figures 27, 28. The thick-and-thin effect is achieved through varying pressure and brush angle. Experiment with it and see what happens. Note how the brush angle and hand position change as I decrease the pressure on the brush.

Figure 28

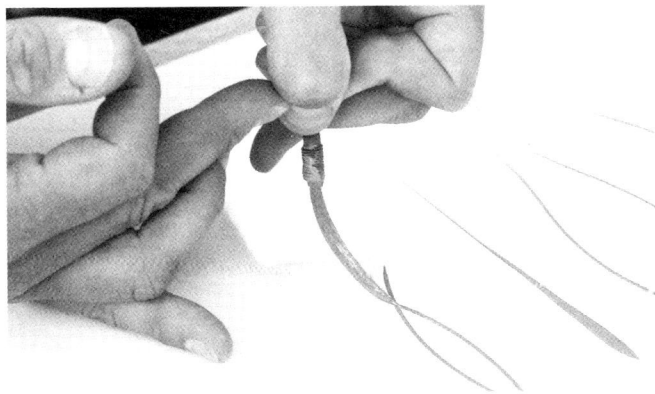

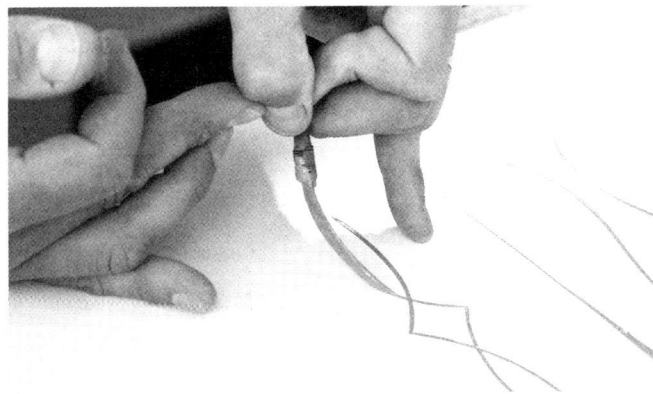

Figures 29, 30. This design is made up of connected and over-lapped single curves.

Figure 30

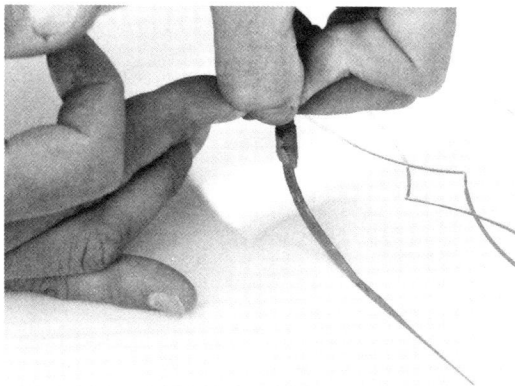

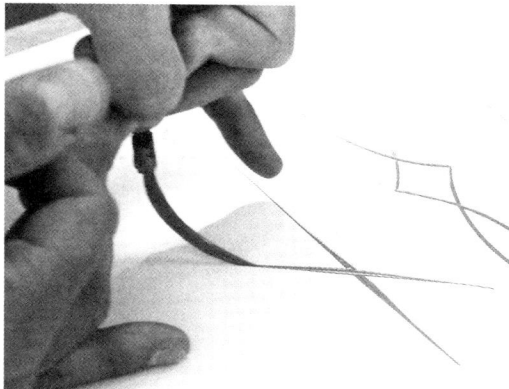

Figure 32

Figures 31, 32, 33. The star is a group of four intersecting thick-and-thins. There's a rumor going around that "real" stripers don't do stars, but it's handy to know anyhow.

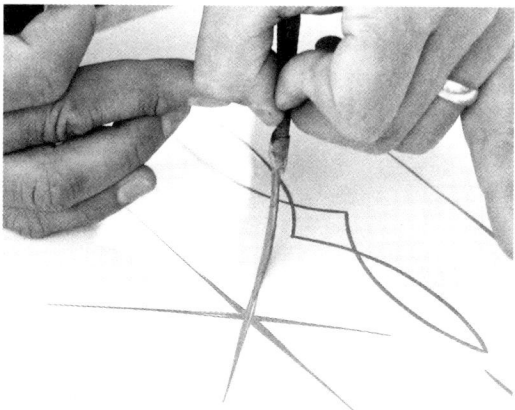

Figure 33

Building a basic design

Now that you have these six moves under your belt, let's build a design.

When I start painting a design, I often only have a vague idea of what it will look like when it's finished. I try to let the design develop as I work my way through it. This spontaneity gives a special feel to the design, I think, and that's what pinstriping is all about.

If you're just starting out, "doodling" on a piece of acrylic sheet or a painted metal panel will probably be very helpful. It allows you to get a feel for what

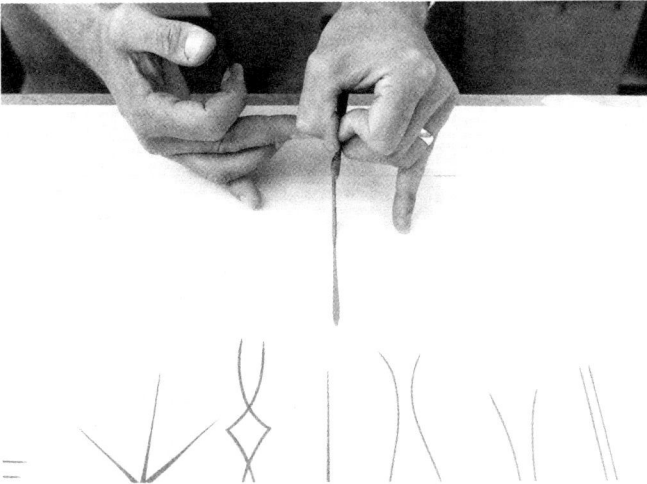

Figure 34

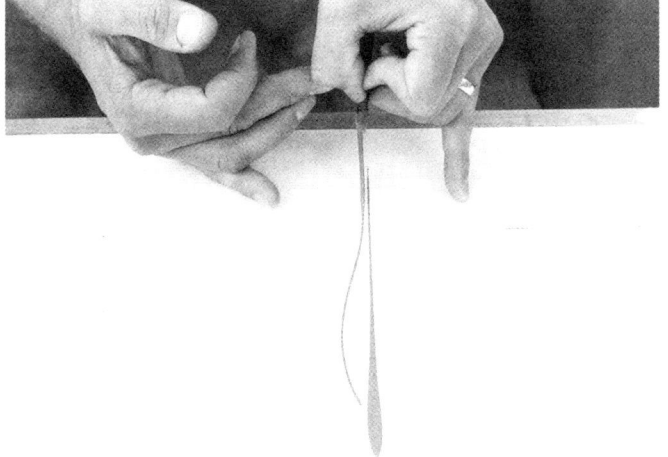

Figure 35

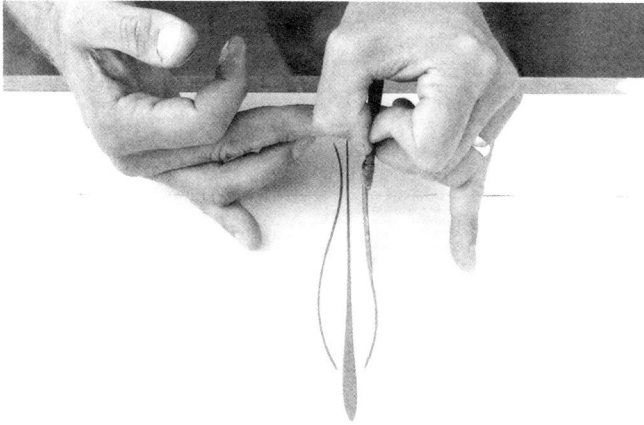

Figure 36

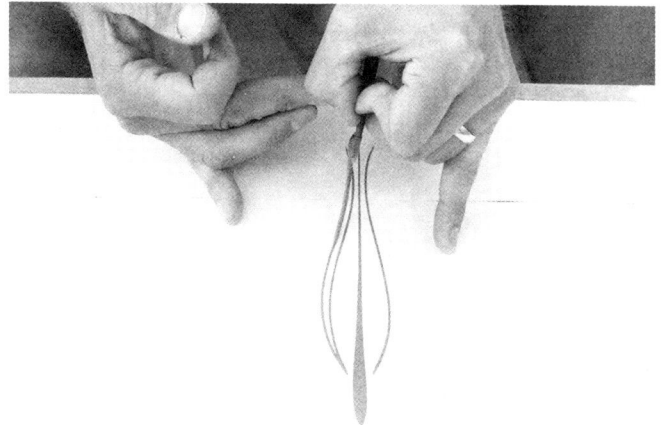

Figure 37

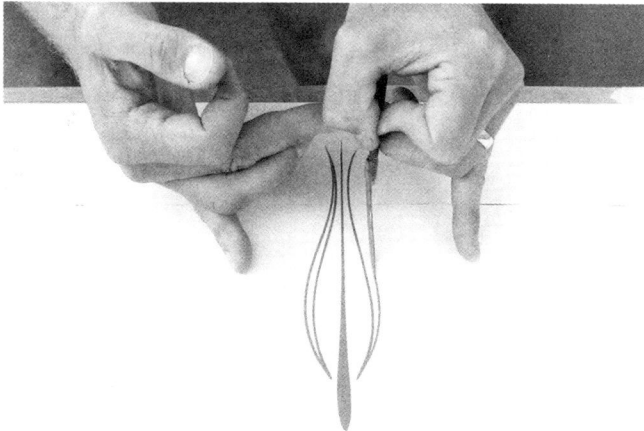

Figure 38

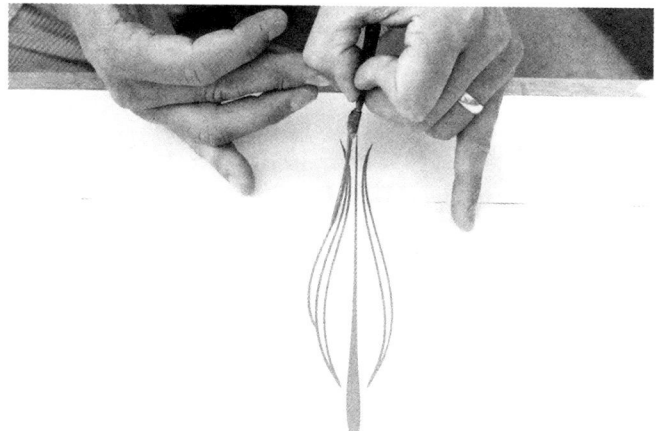

Figure 39

works and what doesn't. When finally start building designs, you may want to sketch a guideline of the general shape of the design. If you feel you need more than a rough sketch, make a pounce pattern. By folding a piece of pattern paper in half and drawing half of the design on it, you can pounce through both layers of paper and have a near-perfect pattern to work from.

Most of my designs evolve as they go together, even though I may do some planning ahead of time. Do whatever comes naturally as you build a design.

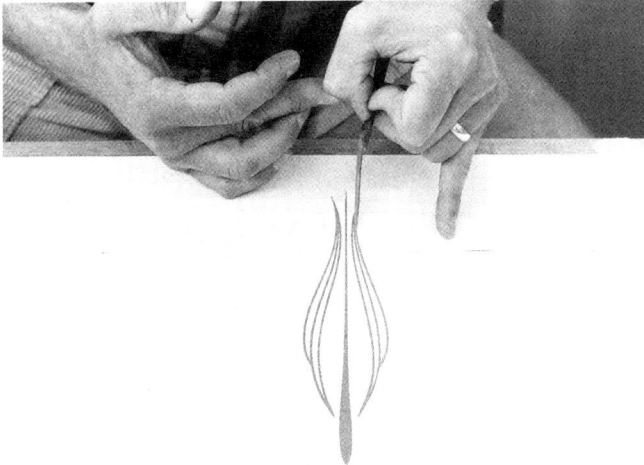

Figure 40

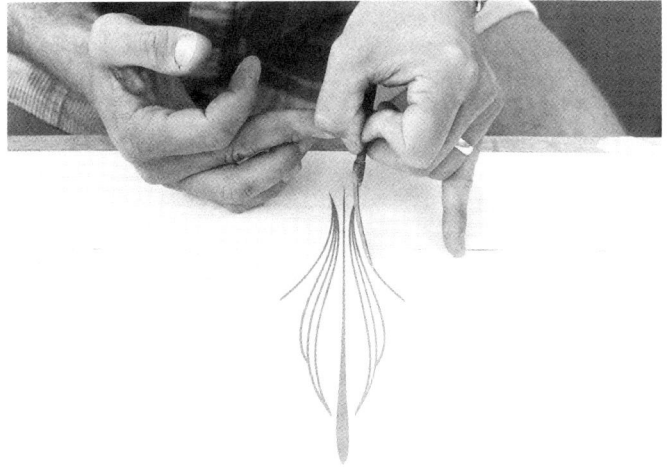

Figure 41

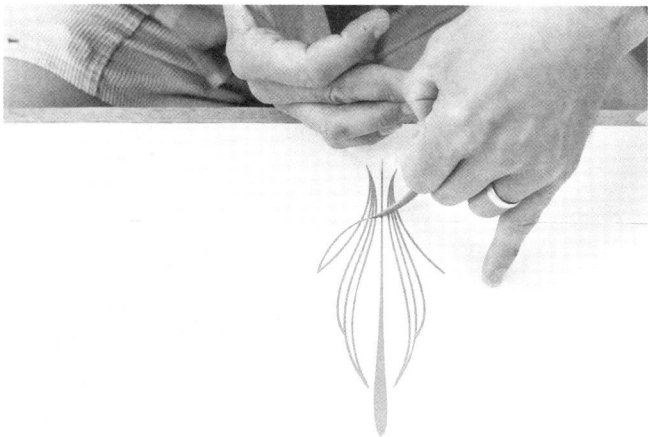

Figure 42

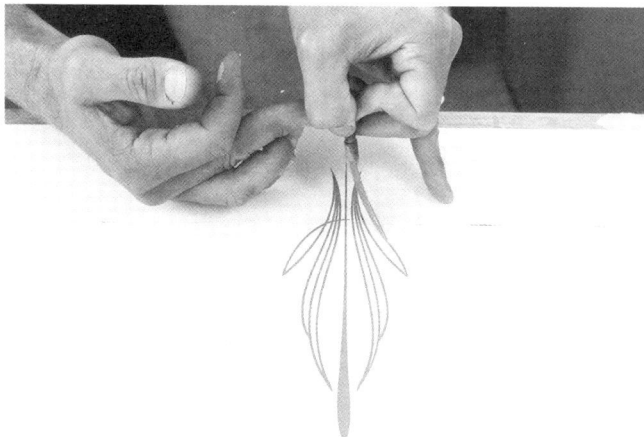

Figure 43

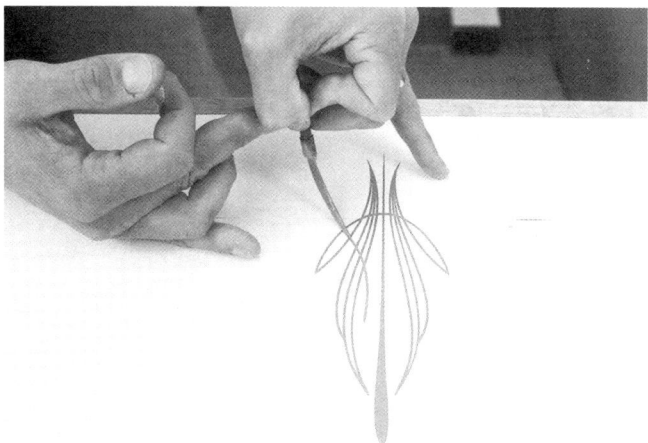

Figure 44

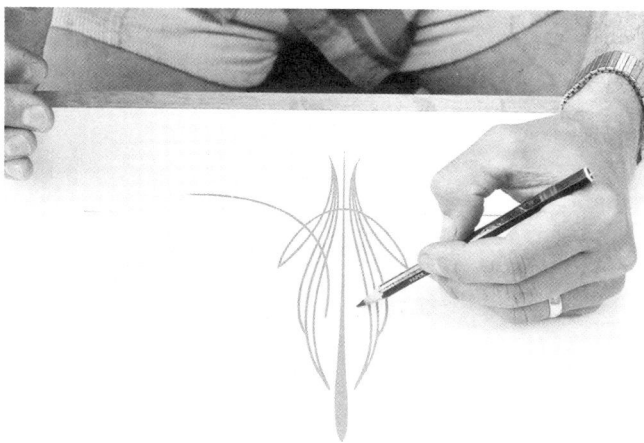

Figure 45

Sometimes your designs will come out great, other times they won't. I'm not beyond wiping off an entire design if I feel it's not quite right or that it's gotten away from me.

The guidelines for the design shown here were simply a vertical and a horizontal centerline. I use a Stabilo No. 8046 for this.

I started this design with a vertical thick-and-thin (Figure 34). A vertical is a good place to start, and embellishing it with a thicker portion adds a nice effect. Next I added a series of reverse curves

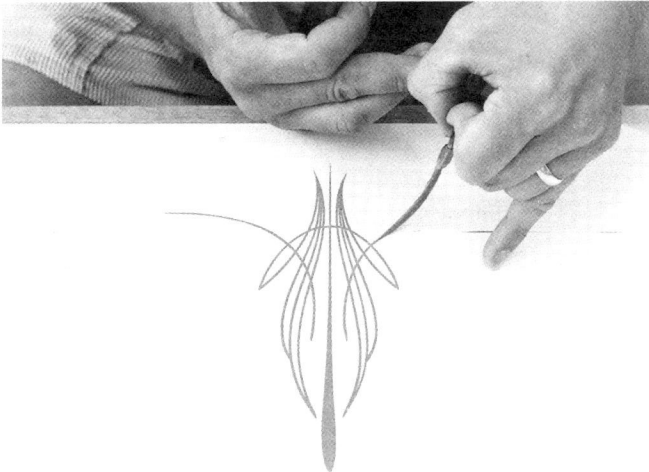

Figure 46

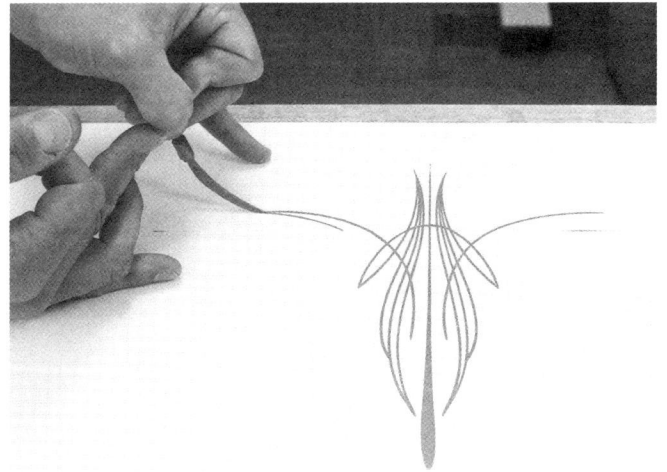

Figure 47

(Figures 35-40), being careful to maintain as much symmetry as possible. (If it helps to pencil in a line before painting it, go right ahead.) After the two connected reverse curves, I added a pair of single curves, one to each side (Figure 41). Starting at the top of each single curve, I pulled another single curve back to the centerline (Figures 42 and 43), taking care that they met evenly. The rest of the design is made up of single and reverse curves. Whenever I feel that a pencil line will help me duplicate a form opposite the original, I always take

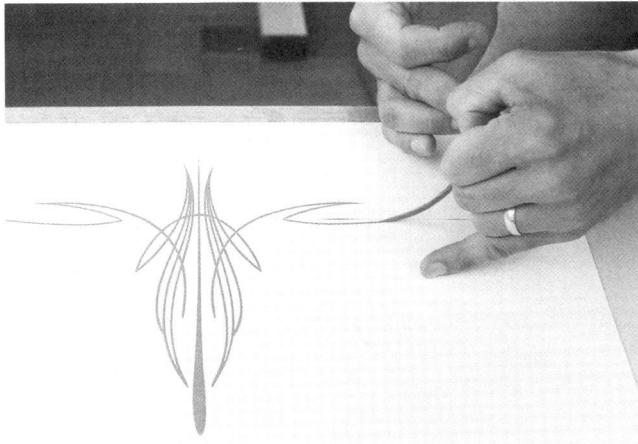

Figure 48

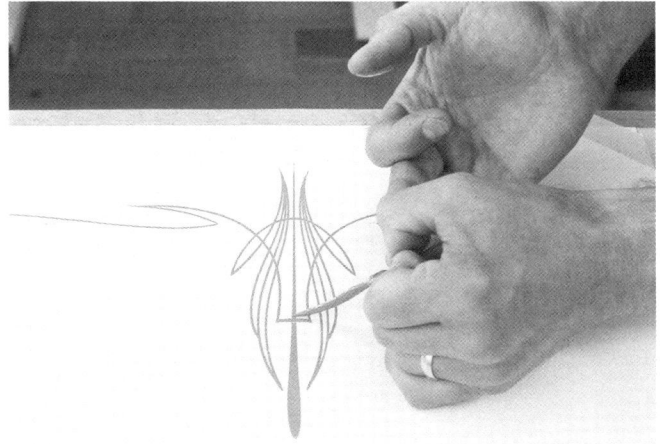

Figure 49

a second to draw it in — usually as a dotted line (Figure 45). Drawing in the corresponding portion on a symmetrical piece achieves greater symmetry and allows you to concentrate on line weight.

On a symmetrical design, I work back and forth between the two sides so that it doesn't get away from me — I paint one or two strokes on one side, then duplicate them on the other side. I usually paint the right side of the design before I paint the left. If you're right-handed, paint the left side first. Otherwise, your hand may obscure the stroke

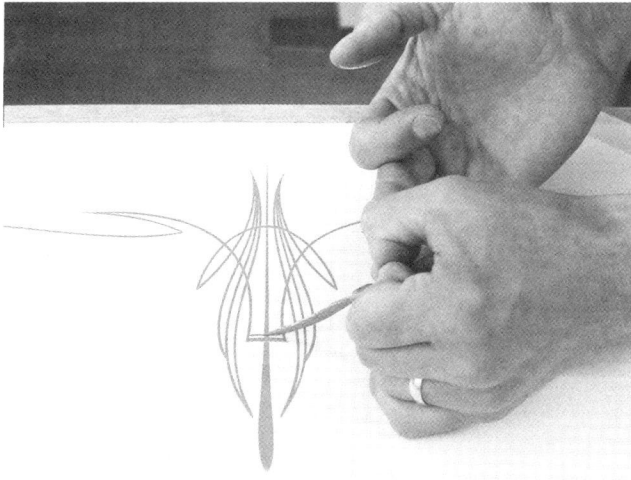

Figure 50

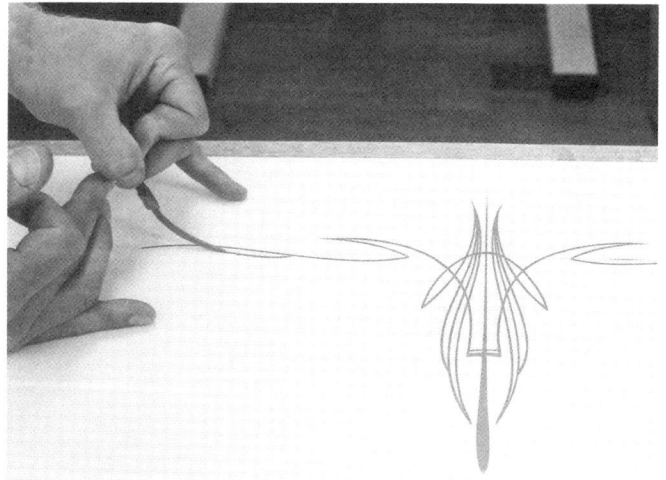

Figure 51

you are trying to duplicate from the other side.

A design like this one (Figure 52) would work well on a bike trailer, a trunk lid, or on one of the large, flat surfaces of a tractor trailer cab.

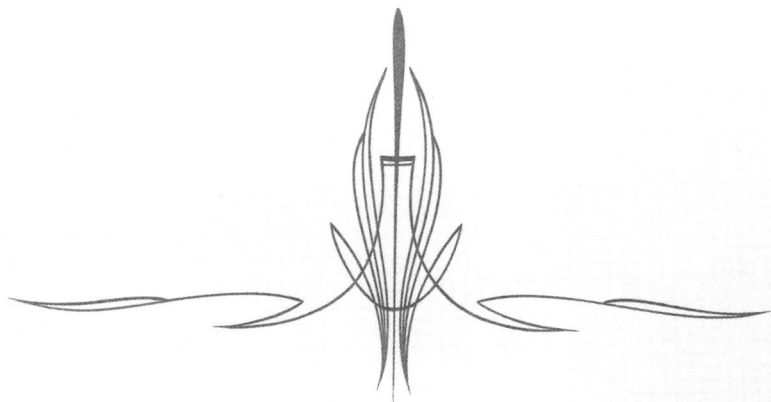

Figure 52

CHAPTER FOUR:
ADVANCED TECHNIQUES

Whether doing very simple designs or complicated "advanced" designs, the process is very much the same — I piece together a series of strokes to produce a pleasing design.

There are two basic hand positions for scroll and decorative work. Figure 53 shows your free hand supporting your brush hand with your middle fingers while your little fingers ride on the work surface. Figure 54 shows the hand-over-hand position. Other hand positions are simply variations on these.

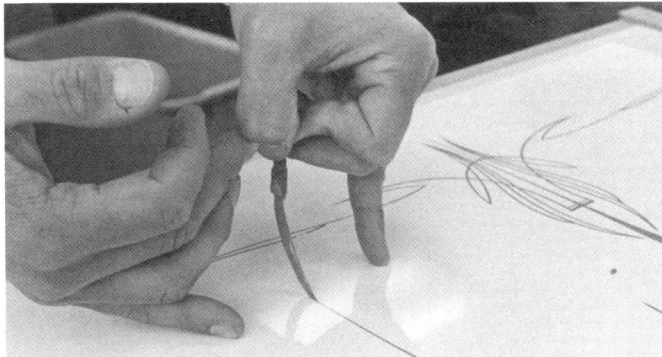

Figure 53

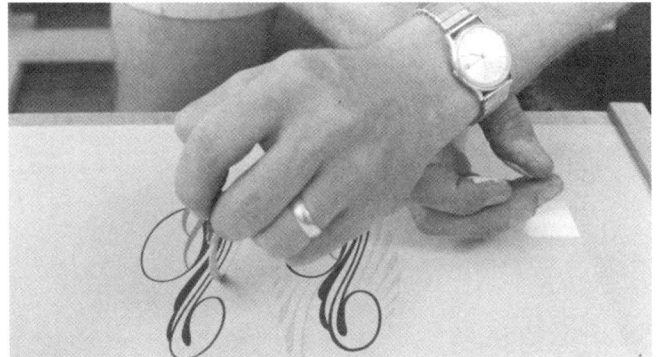

Figure 54

Scrolls and decorative striping

On the following pages, we'll go through several different scroll designs so that you can see how they're built. Of course, there isn't a single "right" way to build a design, but this shows how I would do them. We'll even do one design with two different brushes to show how you can get similar results with different methods.

Step-by-step: Scroll design

This design builds on the basic designs from the previous chapter.

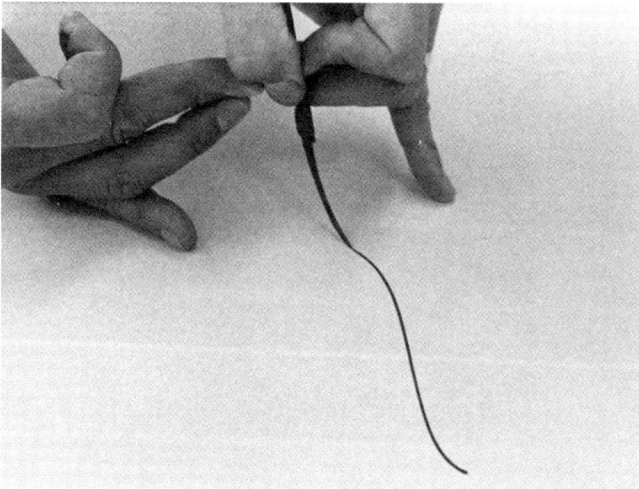

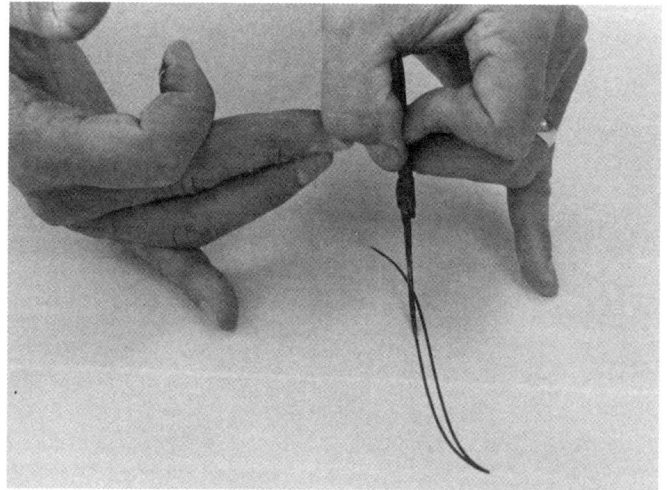

Figures 55, 56. I start out with a series of reverse curves. This creates a very generic "wing" shape.

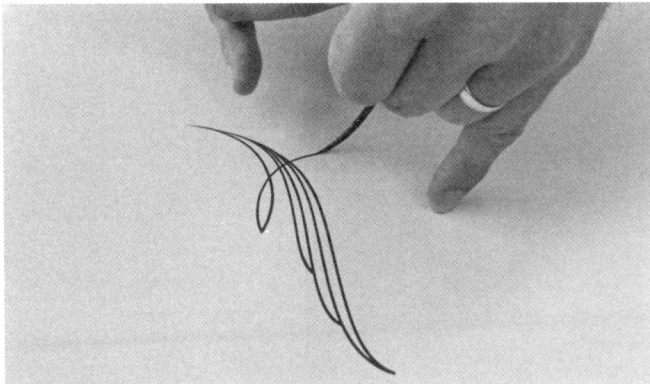

Figure 57. Now I add a little "cross-over" move.

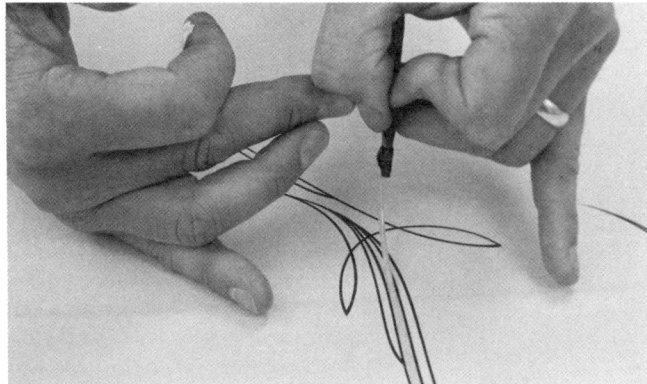

Figure 58. Here a second color is introduced. Adding a second color requires some care — if you make a mistake, it may involve the first color you applied. Fixing such problems can get complicated, so allow the first color a few minutes to dry.

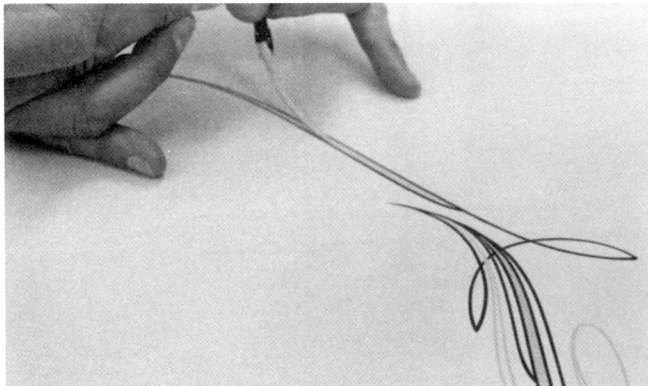

Figure 59. Filling in

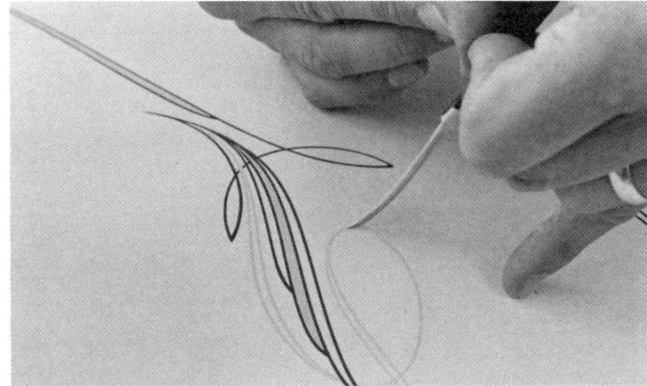

Figure 60. To finish this design, I'll add some scroll work. I used a sword striper in this case, but could have used an outliner.

Step-by-step: Symmetrical design

A design like this one would work well on a flat surface, like a trunk lid or motorcycle pull-behind trailer. I chose to demonstrate this design because it includes a filled-in teardrop, which is a popular effect.

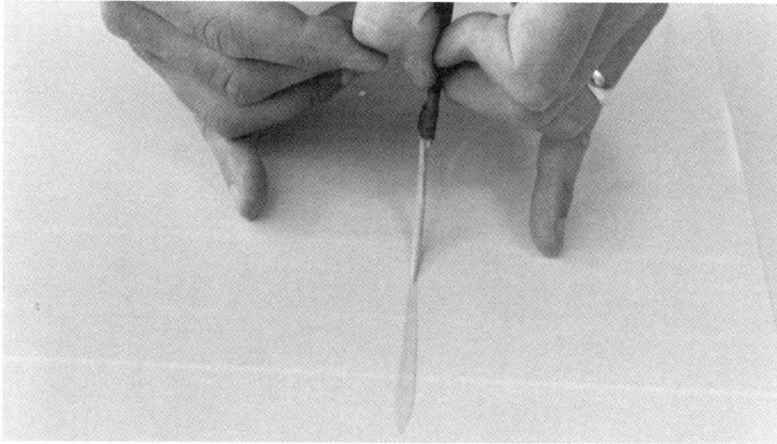

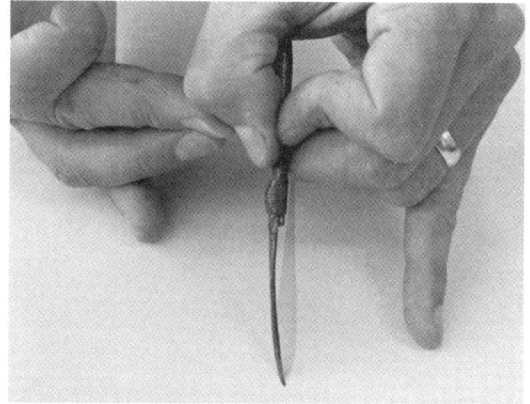

Figure 61. I start by painting a solid teardrop shape (the "thick-and-thin" from the previous chapter) with the lighter secondary color. Actually, either color could have been used.

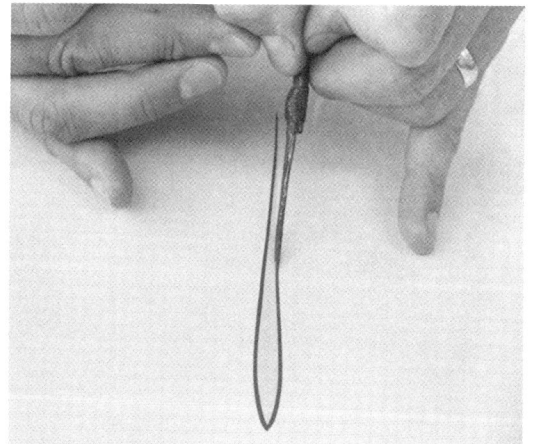

Figures 62, 63. After the paint has dried a little, I add an outline to that shape.

Figure 66. After the primary color has dried a bit, I go back and finish the design with the secondary color.

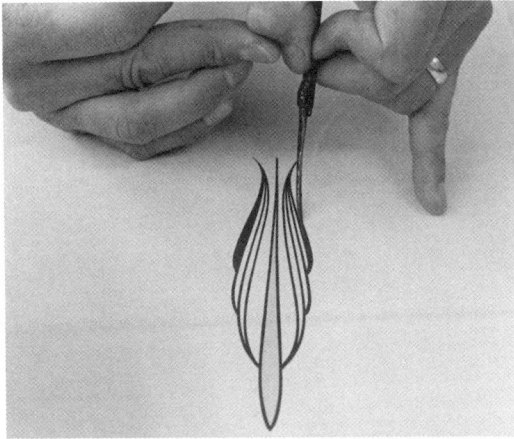

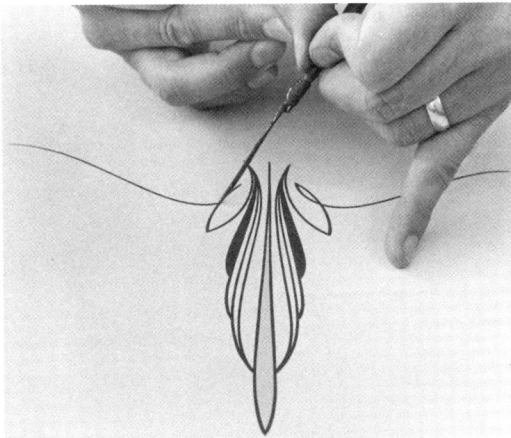

Figures 64, 65. Now I simply build on this center shape.

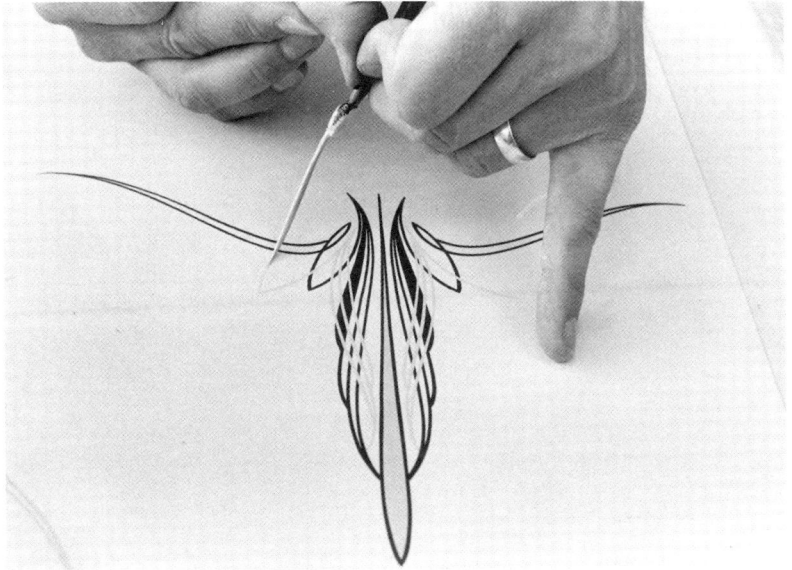

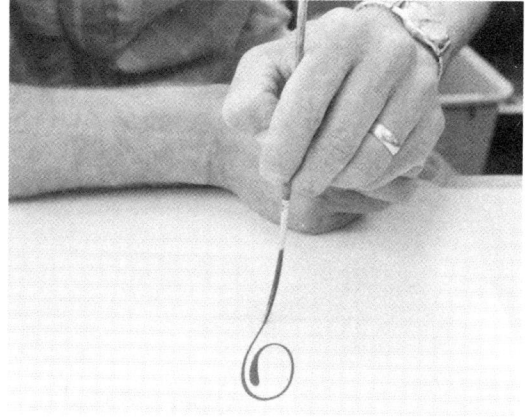

One scroll done two ways

This series of photos illustrates that the same scroll design can be executed with either a radically trimmed Mack 00 striping sword or an outliner.

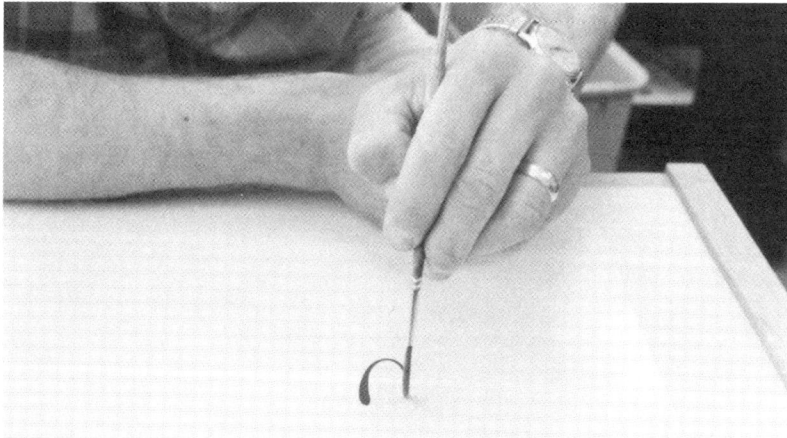

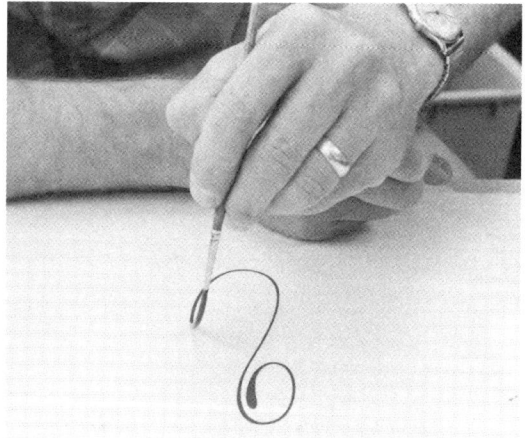

Figures 67-71. I am using a Dick Blick Masterstroke Series 4901 outliner to paint this design. Notice that I'm working hand-over-hand. I start by pressing down at the beginning, lifting in the middle, and pressing down again at the end of the initial stroke. Remember — don't roll the brush between your fingers; just let the hairs twist up.

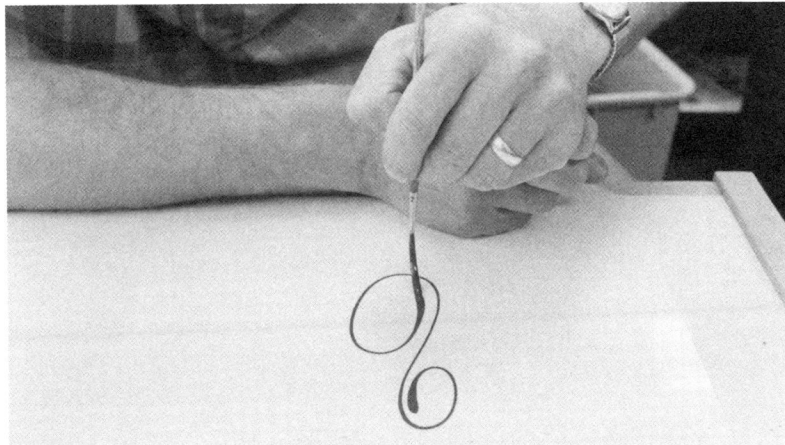

Figure 70

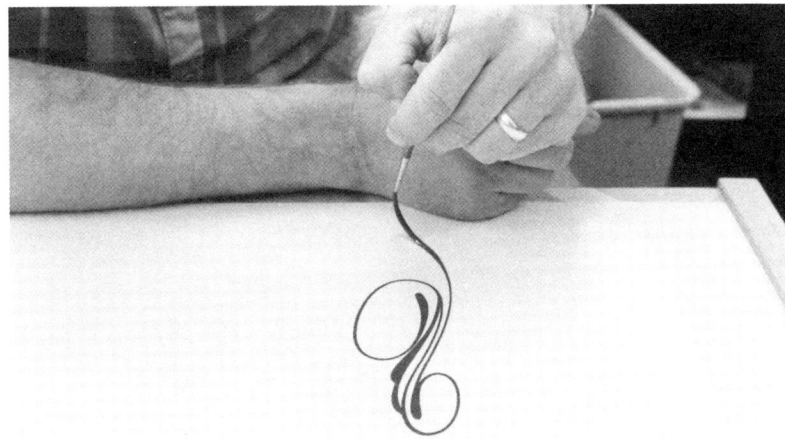

Figure 71

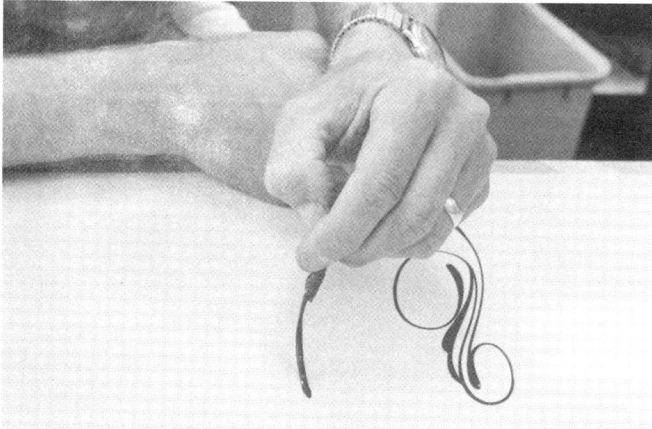

Figures 72-78. Now I execute the same design with a radically trimmed Mack 00 striper.

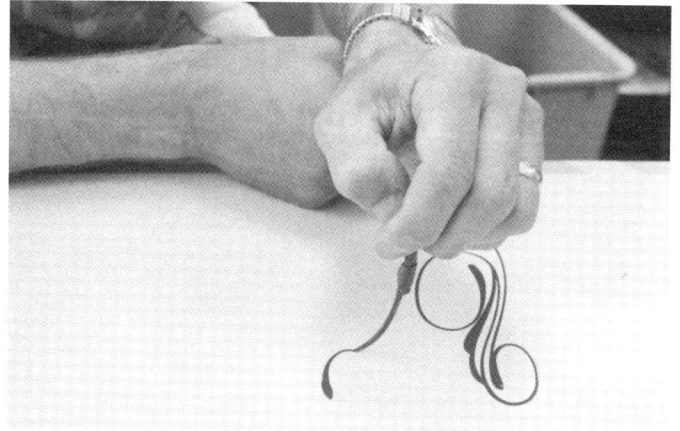

Figure 73

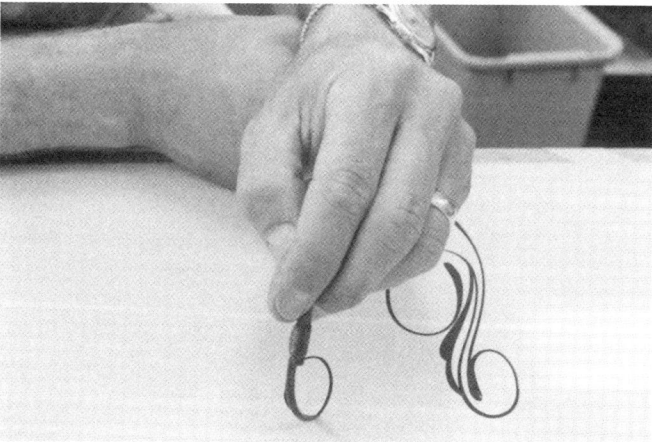

Figure 74

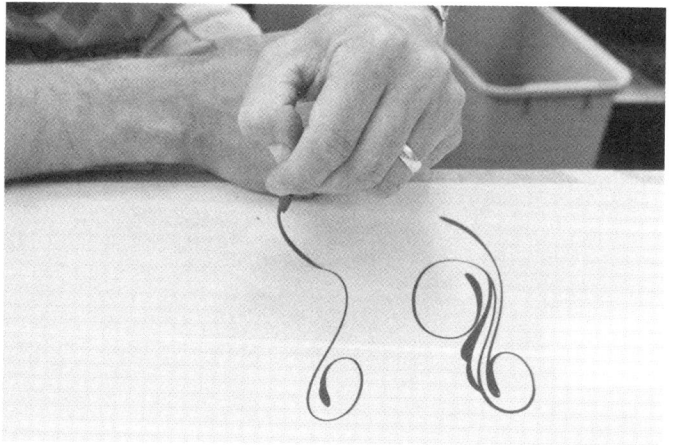

Figure 75

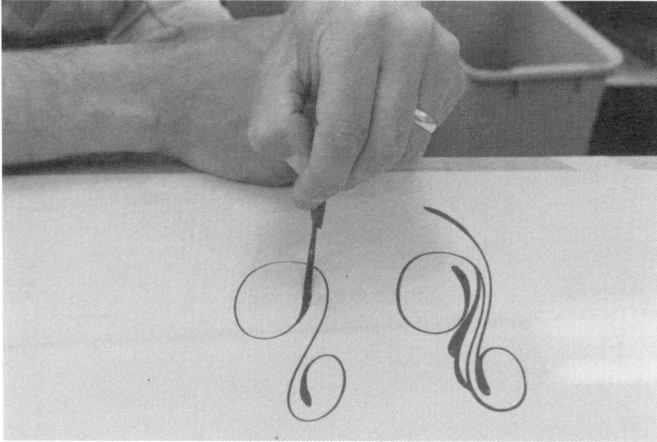

Figure 76

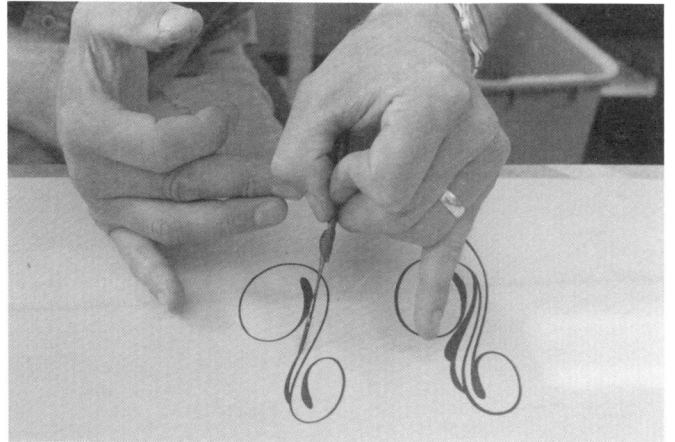

Figure 77

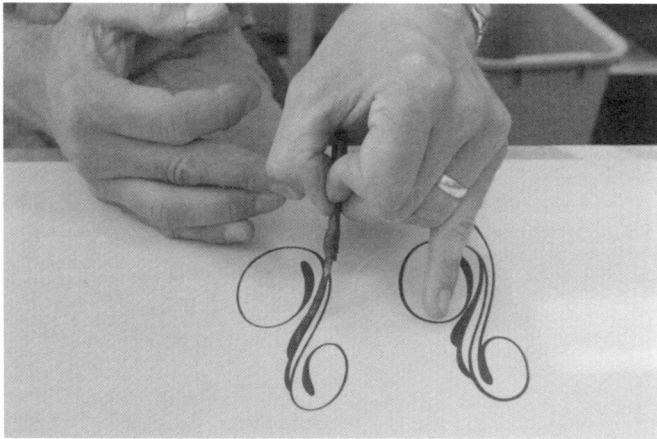

Figure 78

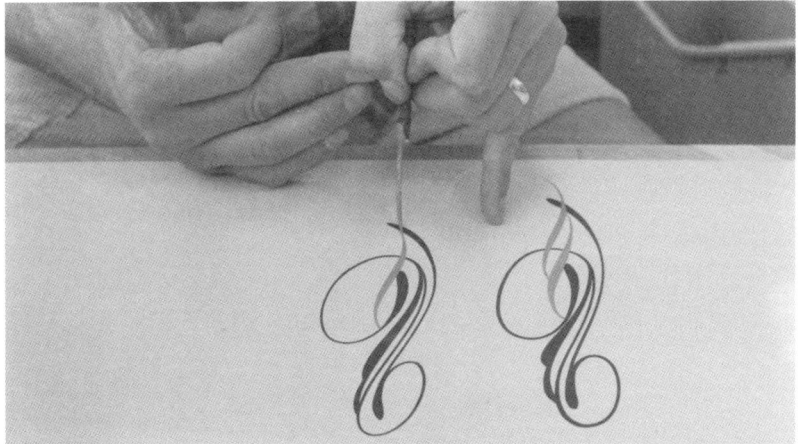

Figure 79. Here I add thick-and-thin reverse curve strokes in a second color.

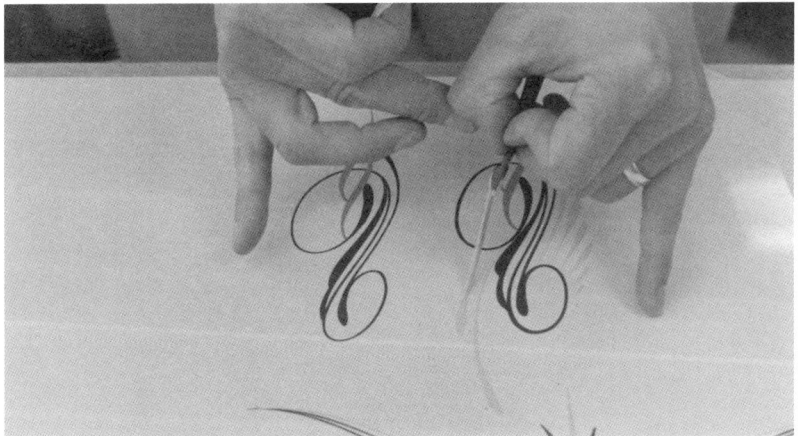

Figure 80. I finish off the design with some "feather" or teardrop shapes.

Step-by-step: Another scroll design

An asymmetrical design like this one would work well on the side panels of a motorcycle, for instance.

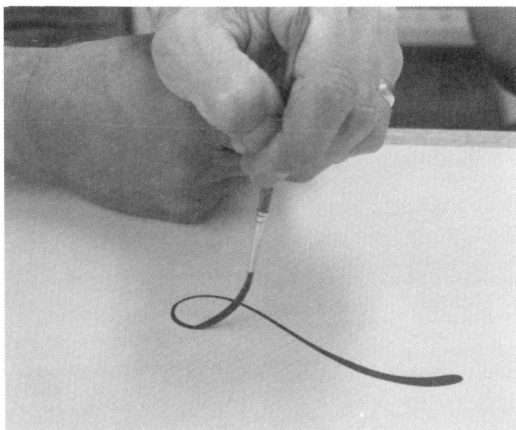

Figures 81, 82, and 83. I start this design by painting the central scroll body of the design with the same outliner I used in the previous demonstration.

Figure 82

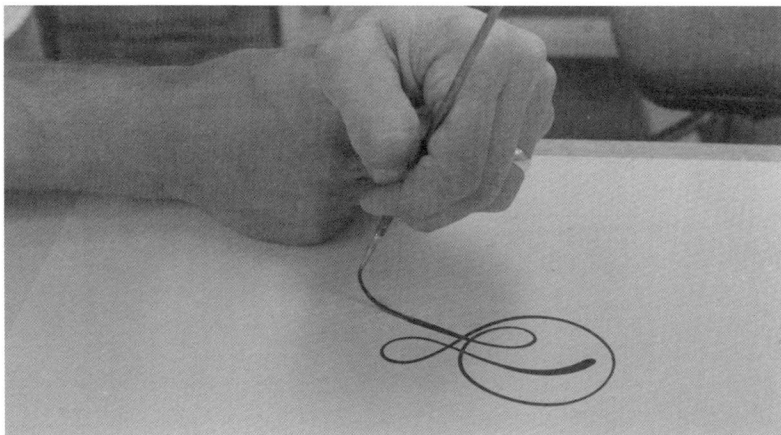

Figure 83

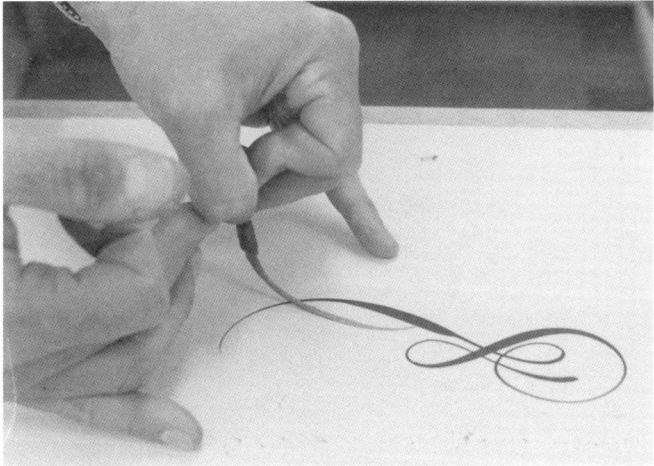

Figures 84 and 85. Now I switch to the sword striper. I have found that when I'm doing a thick-and-thin reverse curve like this one, it helps to slightly roll the brush on its side in the middle (widest) part of the curve. Rolling the brush, along with adding a little extra pressure, makes it easy to execute this stroke in a single pass.

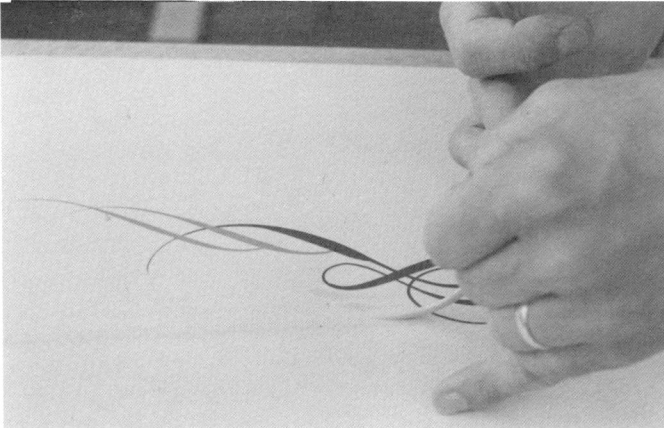

Figures 86-89. I'll add some "feather" strokes, and the design is complete.

Figure 87

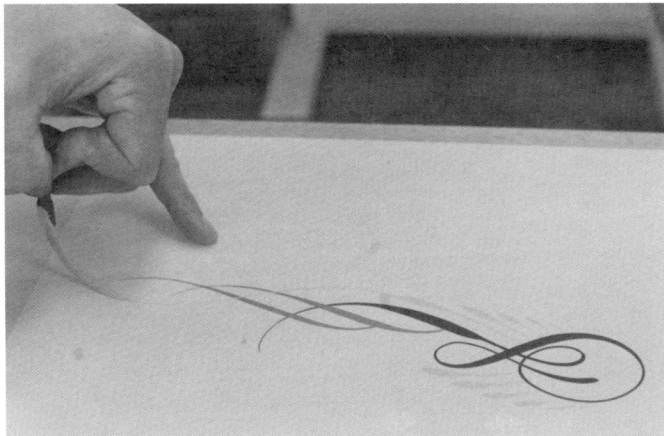

Figure 88

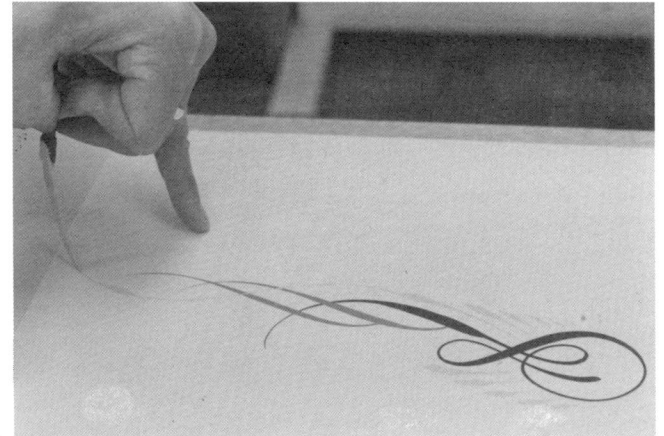

Figure 89

Step-by-step: Script lettering

"How do you get those striping brushes to make such tight circles?" is a question I often hear. Some striping brushes won't make circles at all, but a radically trimmed Mack 00 will do lots of wonderful things. This demonstration illustrates my point. (Note: This design could also be painted with an outliner.)

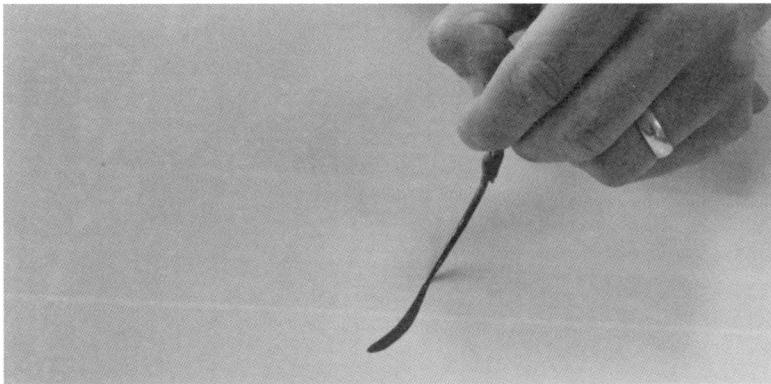

Figure 91. I don't roll the brush between my fingers while doing scroll work. I simply allow the hairs to twist up — it feels like you're dragging a wet noodle around and around.

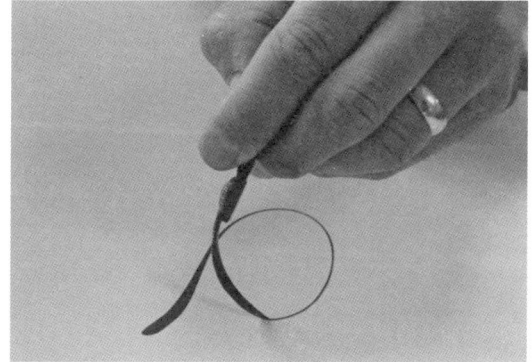

Figure 90. I prefer using a hand-over-hand approach when doing scroll work. I start out by pressing down on the brush (which gives a wider stroke), then I lift the brush as I pull the stroke.

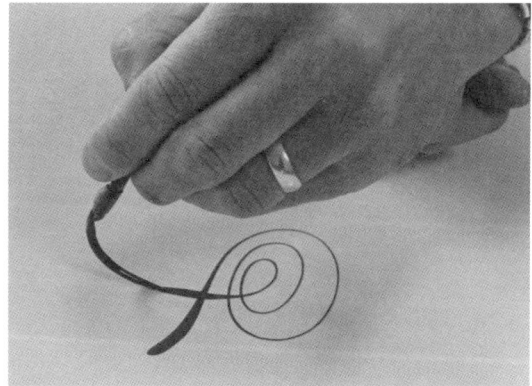

Figure 92. I finish the stroke by pressing down again, then by lifting. It's important to execute strokes like this in one smooth, continuous motion.

Figures 93-96. I do all the lowercase script letters with downstrokes.

Figure 94

Figure 95. I'll finish off the tail of the lowercase "y" with some scroll work.

Figure 96. Quotation marks are a breeze with either a striper or an outliner.

CHAPTER FIVE: SPECIAL EFFECTS

If someone had come up to me 10 or 20 years ago and told me that I'd be splattering and sponging enamel paint onto brand new cars and hot rods (owned by gray-haired grandmas and grandpas, at that), I would have thought they were nuts. But that's going on nearly every day at my shop. Customers of all ages want all kinds of interesting things painted on their vehicles.

This trend has really made my job interesting and challenging. Who knows what's around the corner? Every six months or so, something new seems to pop up.

I hope these next demonstrations will whet your appetite, and help you get started on some projects of your own

Step-by-step: Splatter and blend effects

Like long line striping, I first lay out the design with tape. On this design, I laid down two side-by-side strips of Finesse F-12 tape, and left an ⅛" space between. This created five straight and perfectly spaced lines. Then I laid out the rest of the design with ¼" and ⅛" masking tape (Figure 97).

Figure 97

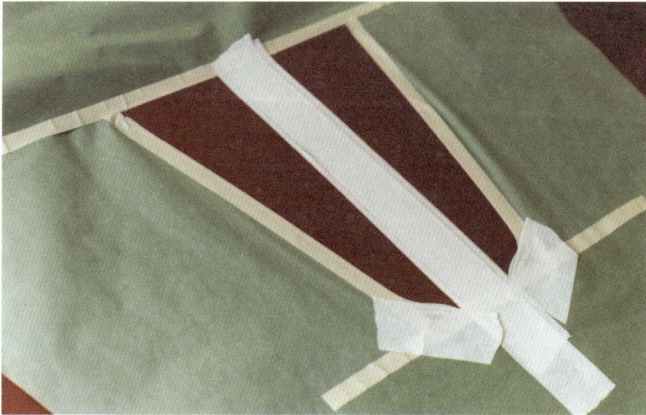

Figure 98. Using paper and masking tape, I mask off the area that I will splatter.

Figure 99. I usually use metal-handled "acid brushes" like the ones shown here, for splattering. Plastic forks and spoons, popsicle sticks, and various brushes can also be used.

Figure 100. Stand back! The harder the flick, the wilder the splatter.

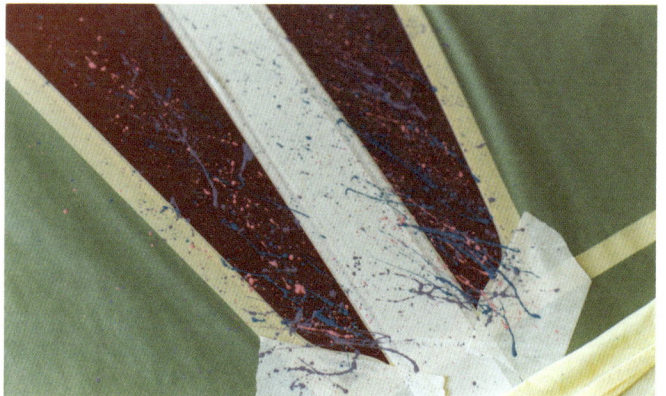

Figure 101. The finished splatter, before I removed the masking.

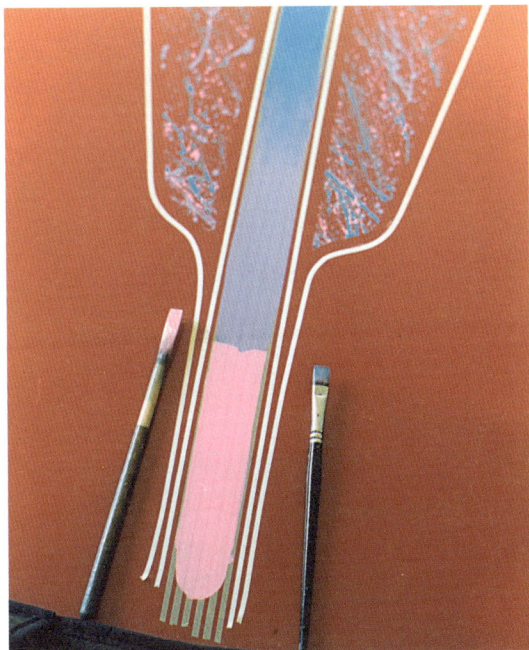

Figure 102. Now on to the blend. On this particular project there are two blends — turquoise to lavender, then lavender to pink. In this photo, the turquoise-to-lavender blend is complete. I start the next blend by painting the lavender right up against the pink.

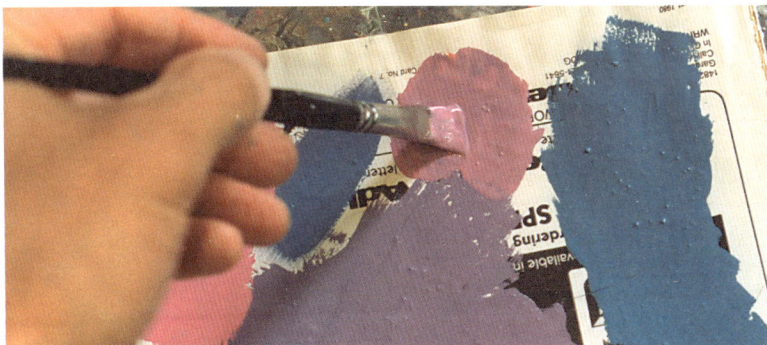

Figure 103. Using a short-haired synthetic flat brush ($4.00 at the art store), I mix equal amounts of the two colors on the palette.

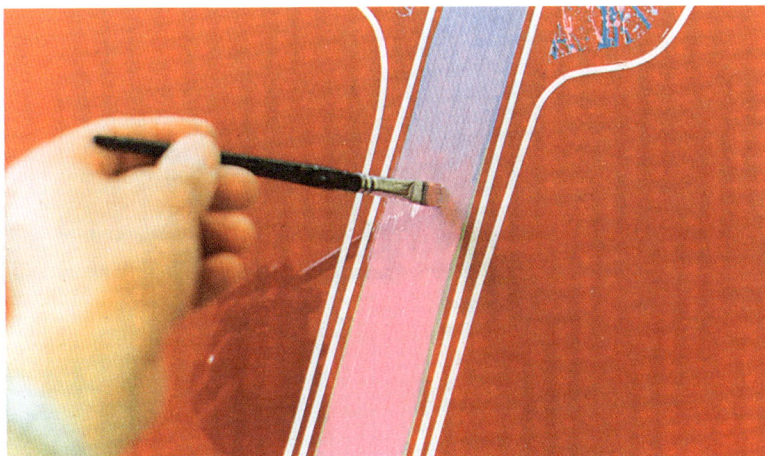

Figure 104. Now using the short back-and-forth strokes and the color I just mixed, I blend the two colors together. This technique produces a nice blend, and only takes a few minutes.

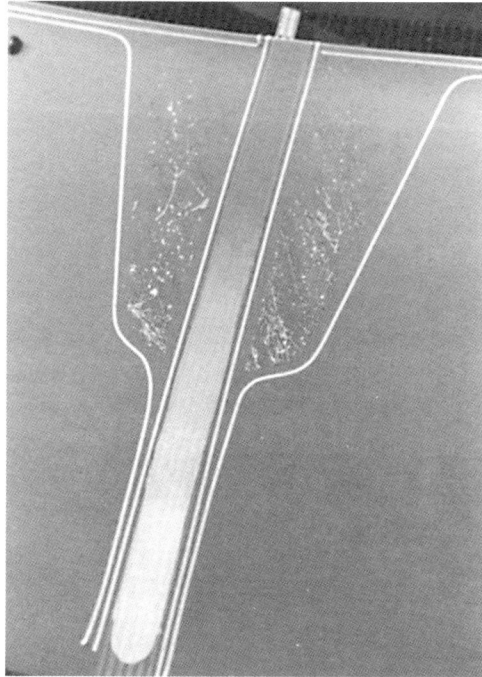

Figure 105. The completed blend, before removing the tape

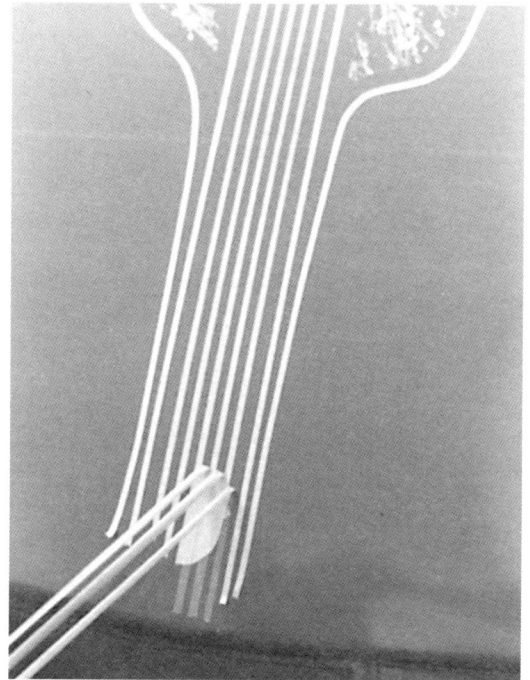

Figure 106. Give the paint a few minutes to tack up, then remove the tape. If any paint has bled out under the tape, now is the time to go back and touch it up. When done properly, the blend looks as if it had been sprayed, not brushed.

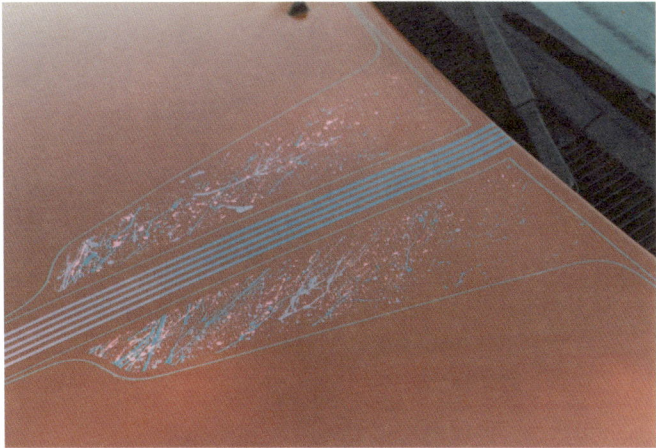

Figure 107. The completed design

Figure 108. Side view of the same vehicle

Figure 109. A shot of the back. Splatter, straight line, a small design by the license tag, and some quick script are all working together.

Step-by-step: Dry brush graphics

"Dry brush" work has been quite popular for the past few years, and I don't think we'll see it fade in popularity any time soon. It really hits the spot on new cars and trucks, and euro-style bikes. It's simple to do (once you get the hang of it), and the sky is the limit design-wise.

Never thin the paint when doing dry brush work. I palette the paint until it becomes very sticky, then holding the brush overhand style between my first finger and thumb, I lightly drag the brush across the surface. Different shapes come from varying the pressure on the brush.

An example of John's dry brush work

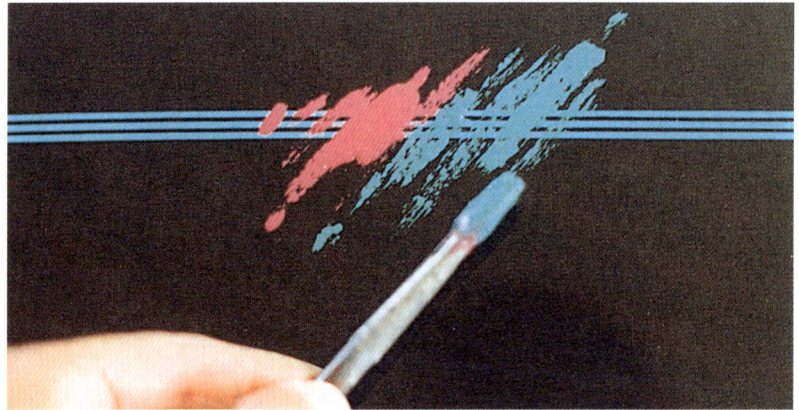

Figure 110. For this work, I use the crummiest old painting brush I own. I never oil or clean it very well—this helps keep it bristly and unruly.

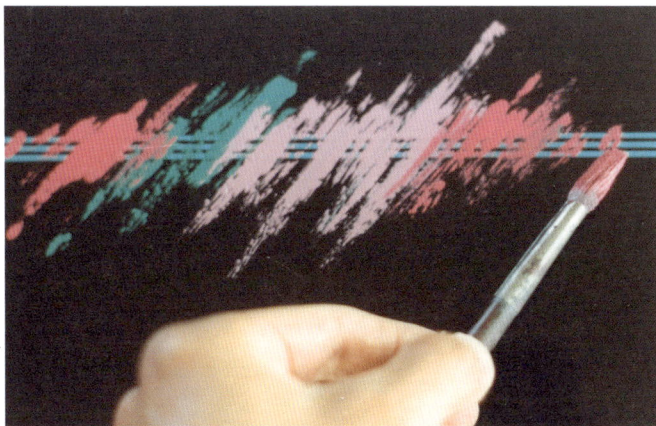

Figure 111. I continue changing colors, and brushing back into the previous color.

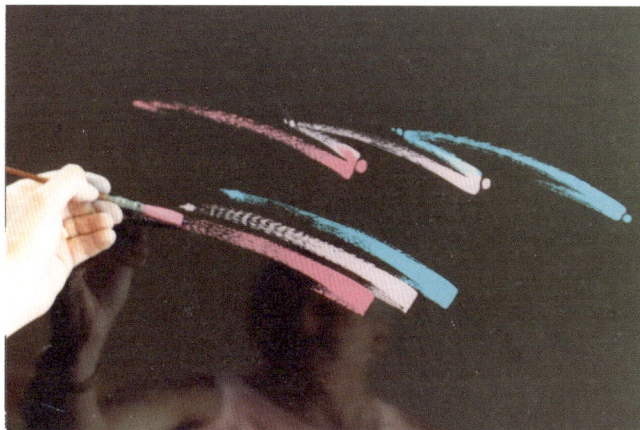

Figure 112. I used a lettering quill held in a more conventional manner to achieve this effect. I start each stroke with normal lettering pressure and lighten up as I pull the stroke. Again, practice and experiment — just about anything goes.

Step-by-step: Sponge and brush highlights

Here's my tray, all set up and ready to go (Figure 113). On this project I'm going to use four different colors in the sponged areas, so I've poured out four puddles of color onto my magazine palette. I've also ripped four 1¼" round sponge balls from the big sponge. I tear off many small pieces of sponge until each ball is kind of round, but with many neat little holes and irregularities.

Figure 113

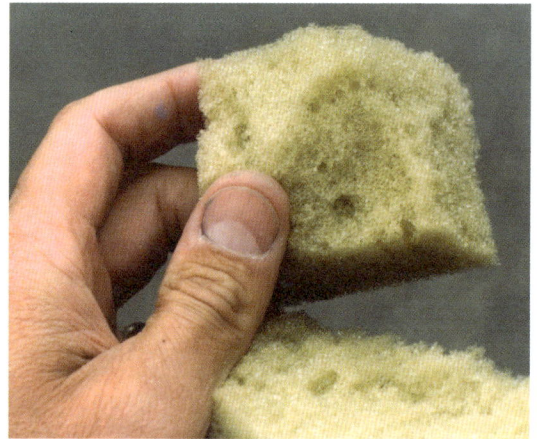

This photo shows the type of sponge I use. It's an inexpensive synthetic sponge from the hardware or grocery store — basically the same sponge you use to wash your car.

Figures 114, 115. I lay out the design with tape. In this case, I used ¼" and ¾" masking tape — ¼" No. 218 Fine Line tape (by Scotch), and ⅛" Scotch No. 471 blue plastic tape.

Figure 116. Now the fun starts! Notice that I've added a piece of ¾" masking tape above and below the layout tape — this serves as "masking", and protects the vehicle's paint when the sponging starts. I put down the pink first, then overlapped it with the blue — which is the next color in the stripe. You don't have to wait for anything to dry, but be sure to use a different sponge for each color. Leave lots of "holidays" for the background color to show through — that's what gives this technique its special effect. Using this technique, it only takes me about 15 minutes to go around a car.

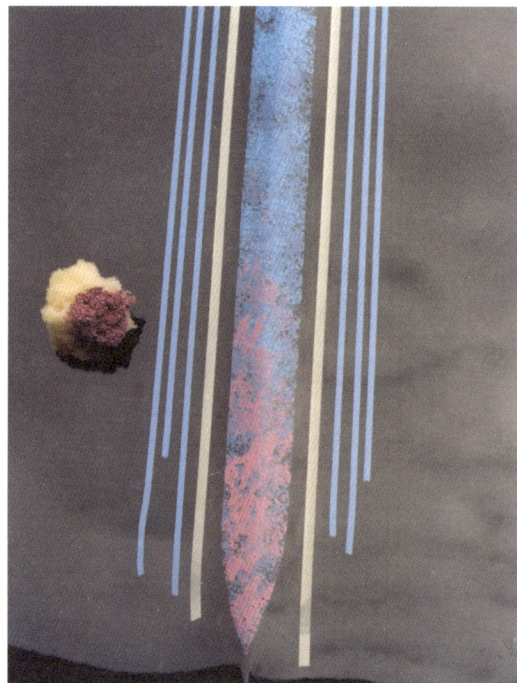

Figure 117. This is the center section of the hood with the masking removed. It could be outlined or even splattered for a different effect.

Figure 118. The finished sponge effect, with other graphics masked off for striping.

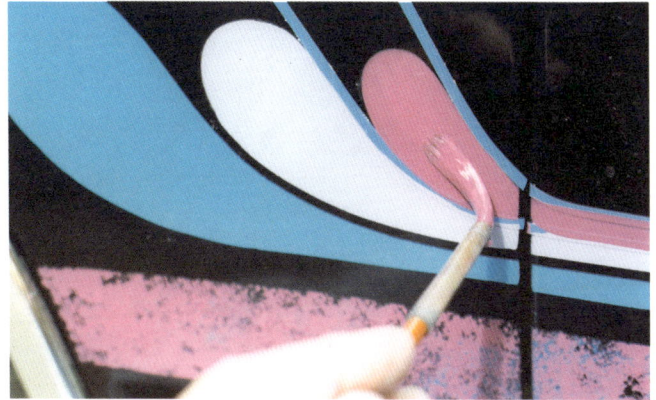
Figure 119. I use a No. 6 lettering quill to fill in the graphic sections.

Figure 120. I brush highlight each section of the graphic with lighter shades of the base color, ultimately ending up with a pure white dot at the end of each highlight point.

Figure 121. The finished door panel with striping added

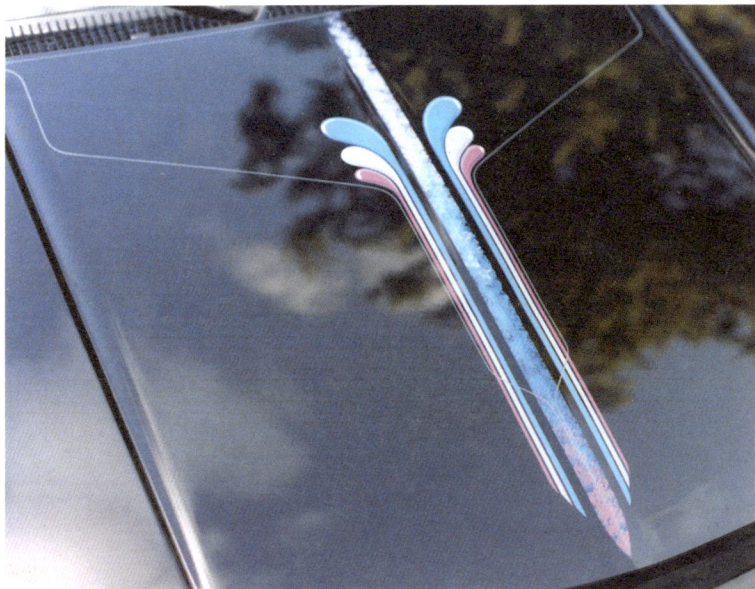

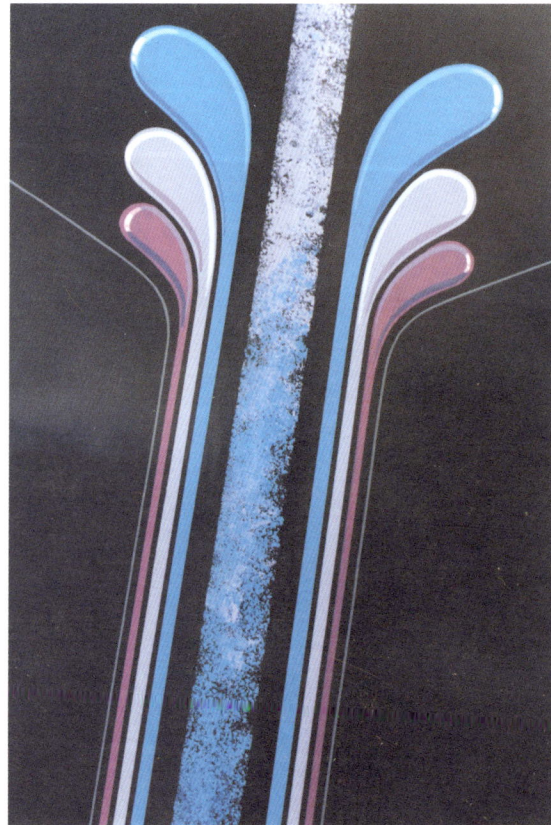

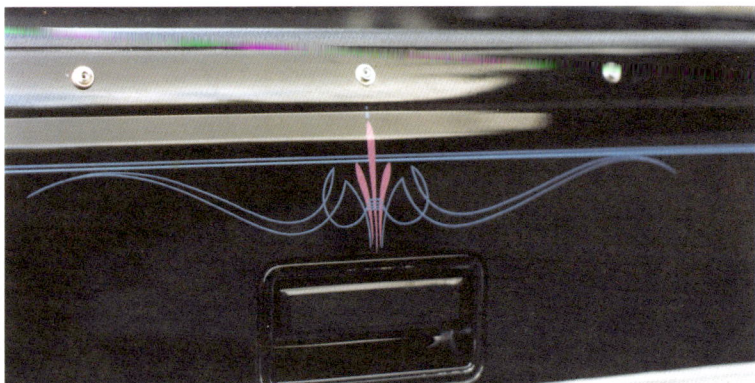

Detail shots

Airbrush highlights on brushed-on graphics

There are a few different ways to high-light a letter or graphic. Probably the most effective and slickest-looking method is by using an airbrush. All of the graphics projects pictured here, with the exception of the photo that shows the gas cap cover, were airbrushed without the use of any frisket paper, or masking.

I do these projects by hand painting the graphics, then while the paint is still wet, I carefully airbrush the highlights and shadows. It doesn't matter if a little lettering enamel overspray gets on the surface of the vehicle — it can be

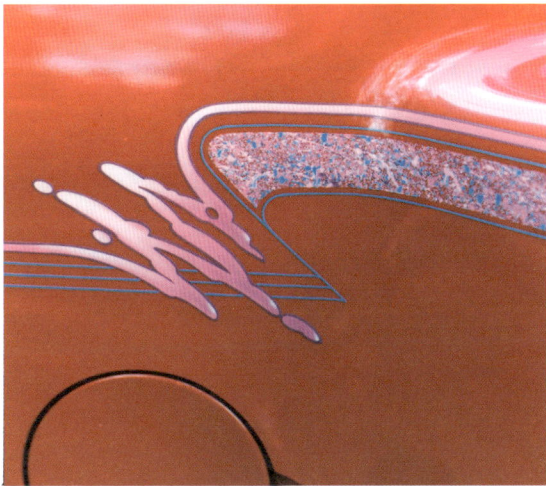

cleaned off the next day with denatured alcohol or household window cleaner. By airbrushing wet-on-wet like this, the colors usually dry to an even gloss and no clear-coat is needed.

I use a Paasche (Paasche Airbrush Co., 7440 W. Lawrence Ave., Harwood Heights, IL 60656) Type H or VL Model airbrush for this work, and thin my paint with mineral spirits or Ditzler Delstar acrylic enamel reducer. (I use DTR-607 in hot weather.) Always wear a respirator when airbrushing paint.

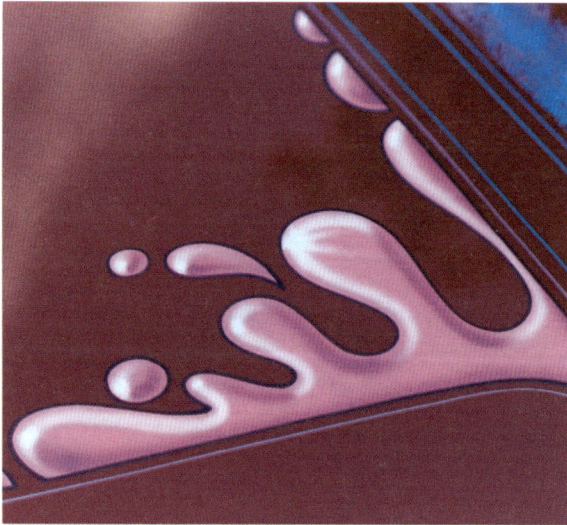

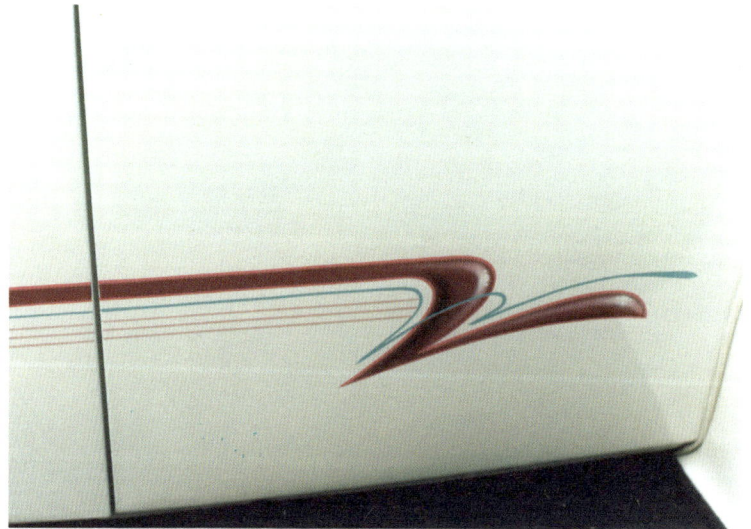

Step-by-step: Cartoons

For as long as I have been painting, it seems there has always been quite a bit of cartoon work to do. Commercial vehicles, cars, trucks, boats, planes, bikes, you name it — they all want cartoons from time to time.

While I was attending college 20 years ago, I worked for two cartoonists/sign painters — Bob Hale and Dick Bell in Seattle, Washington. They taught me a simple and quick method of coloring cartoons that works well on simple and more complex projects. A book full of great cartoon ideas is available from Hale and Bell's Cartoon College, P. O. Box 30083, Seattle, WA 98103. It sells for $14.95.

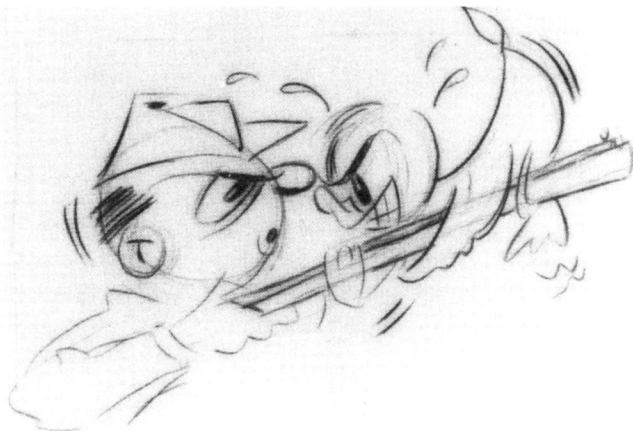

Figure 122. I start by sketching the cartoon with a black Stabilo.

Figure 123. Now for the important part: instead of painting the face solid flesh color, the duck solid yellow, and the clothes solid green, I paint each area in three shades of the color that makes it up. In this example, I'm working as if the light source is coming from the left. This means the light shade of each color falls on the left side of the cartoon, while the medium shade falls in the middle, and the darkest shade on the right.

Figure 124. Now that the paint has dried a little, I'll outline everything in black (using a No. 1 Luco quill). Notice how I vary the line width — this gives the cartoon motion and a spontaneous look. Also, notice the action lines and sweat marks which help add "snap" to the cartoon.

Step-by-step: Roses

If there's one thing that I've painted on a lot of motorcycles over the last few years, it's roses.

Several years ago I noticed that people were asking for painted roses. I tried my hand at them, but they took too long to paint and looked overworked. So I went to the art store and bought a few books on tole painting that showed step-by-step rose painting procedures. (Tole painting is the folk art type of painting that is often used to decorate antique furniture. It originated in Germany and Austria.) I experimented with painting them with lettering enamel and found that it worked.

A rose like this one is about a half hour's work.

Figure 125. I use a small scroller brush for detail, a No. 3 lettering quill for the leaves, and a ½" flat synthetic shader brush for the petals. I also use a small round synthetic brush for blending (see Figure 130) and an outliner for the stem (see Figure 137). I start out with a simple sketch.

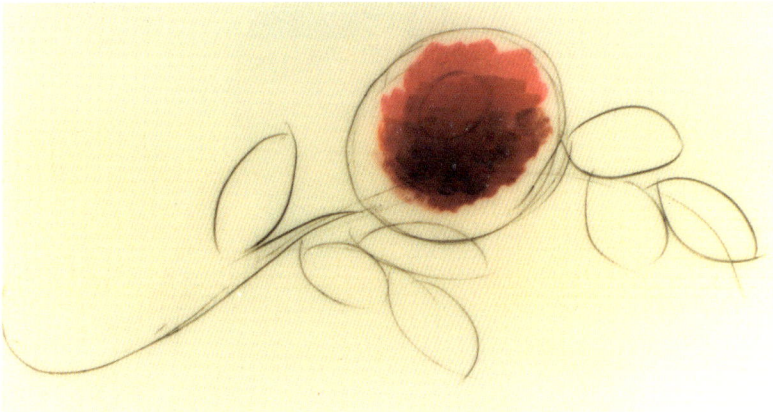

Figure 126. Next I lay in a dark-to-light shaded center section, working from bottom to top.

Figure 127. The key to this technique is that I load the brush with the base color of a petal first, then tip the corner of the brush in white or other light shade of paint (you'll see this technique repeated in Figure 131).

Figure 130. After the third row is finished I take a short-haired brush and blend the bottom of this stroke with the background color.

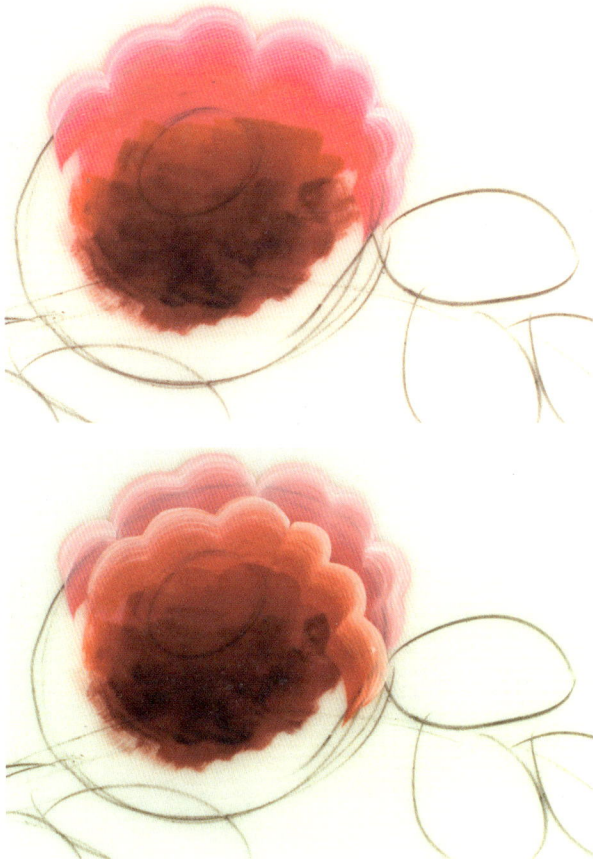

Figure 128, 129. By double-loading a brush like this, each stroke produces a multi-colored petal. I start at the outside of the flower and work row-by-row toward the center.

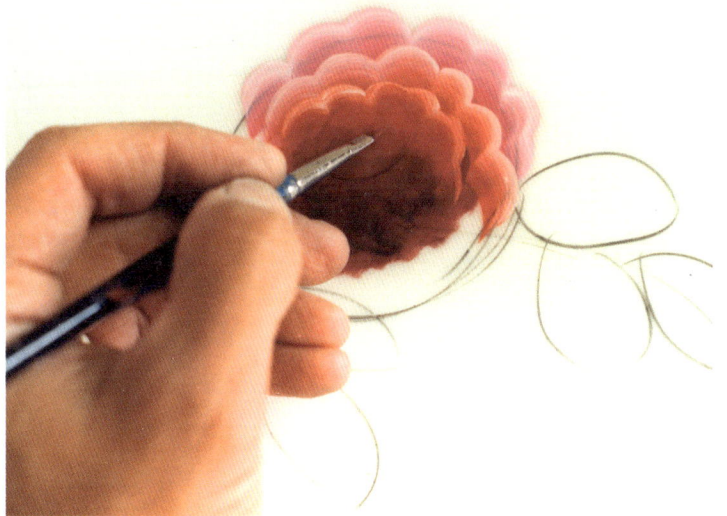

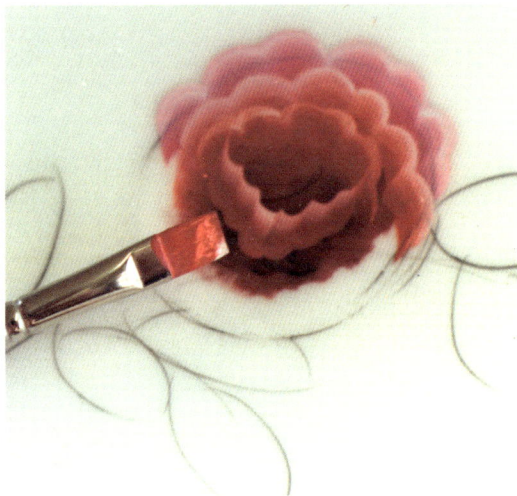

Figure 132. I add another row of petals, then apply the outside petals in the foreground. In this case, I do that by applying the petal on the very bottom first, then overlapping the other two petals slightly. Always change the colors slightly between strokes.

Figure 131. Now I'll add the front side of the center petals.

Figure 133. This photo shows that I've added two more petals.

Figure 134. Now I'll add the last two inner petals. I use the scroller brush to add details to the petal edges.

Figure 136. Using a quill, I add the second — and lightest — color to the leaves.

Figure 135. Next I add stamens to the center of the rose, and lay down the first (and darkest) color of the three-colored leaves.

Figure 137. *Using the scroller brush, I add leaf and stem details. I used an outliner for the heavy part of the stem. You can also see that I've added the second and third colors to the leaves.*

Figure 138. *The finished product with all the little details touched up and the Stabilo marks removed*

I sell these roses for $65 each or $600 a dozen.

Step-by-step: Pictorials

There are times when a customer will want something that requires more than a "cartoon approach" painted on their vehicle. Wildlife, outdoor, and floral scenes all need to be approached from the standpoint of realism. My interest in watercolor and oil painting has helped me in this regard. There are several books available on this subject, and if you intend to market this type of work, I recommend studying a few of them.

In the case of this project, the customer wanted a white tiger painted on the hood of the vehicle.

Figure 139. I start by freehanding the sketch with a Stabilo pencil (I work right on the surface of the vehicle).

Figure 140. Since this is a light subject on a light background, I sponge around the outside of the subject with lavender, blue, and white enamel.

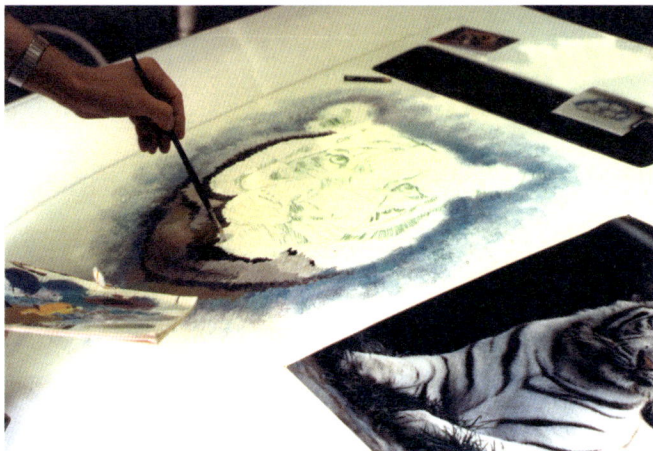

Figure 142. Here I'm about halfway done. This is about 1½ hour's work.

Figure 141. Using a short, round tip, soft hair brush, I begin painting the animal's hair. Remember that when painting fur, hair, or feathers, always work from the background to the foreground, overlapping the strokes as you go. I lay out small puddles of paint on a palette and work the pictorial "oil painting style," mixing and painting as I go. As a rule of thumb, slightly change the color in your brush every six strokes or so. This helps give a more realistic look.

Figure 143. Moving along. I save the best part — the eyes — till last.

Figure 144. Finished except for the eyes and whiskers

Figure 145. Now I paint in the eyes with a smaller brush.

Figure 146. Using a striping sword, I paint in the whiskers.

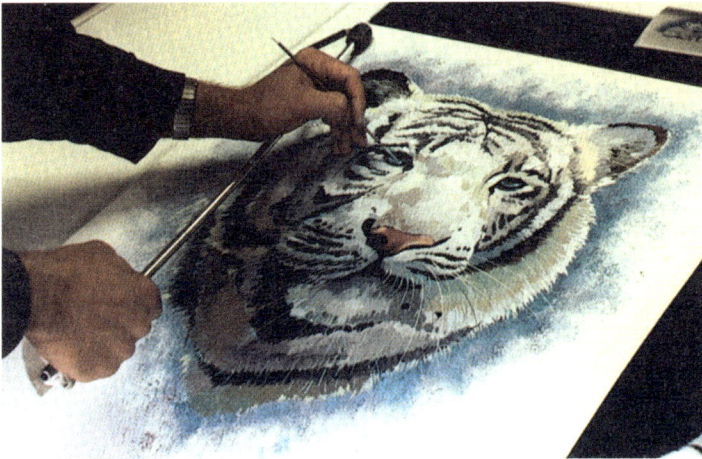

Figure 147. Adding the highlight to the eye

Figure 148. The finished product with a reference photo. I almost never clear coat these projects. Granted, this technique leaves a textured surface. But after they've been waxed a few times, they look fine. My customers are almost always tickled, and a project like this one only takes about three hours.

The following pages show a little of my work along with the work of a few of the country's top pinstripers. I would have liked to include all the photos I received, but the limitations of space made that impossible. There are many terrific stripers out there — indeed, one could fill an entire volume with photos of their work. I'd like to thank the artists who took the time to submit photos. Thanks, too, to all the innovative stripers who pioneered the way for today's pinstriping artists. What follows are ten different stripers, and ten distinct pinstriping styles. Take what you see here and run with it, and let your own style evolve.

CHAPTER SIX: GALLERY

John Hannukaine, *Hannukaine Signs & Graphics, Tumwater, Washington*

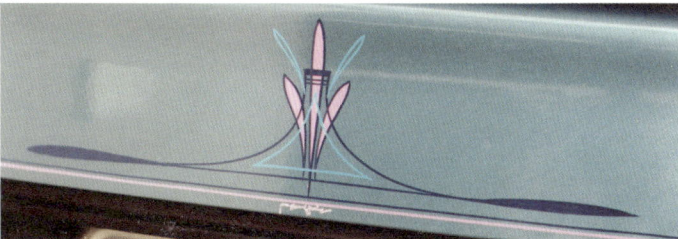

John Hannukaine

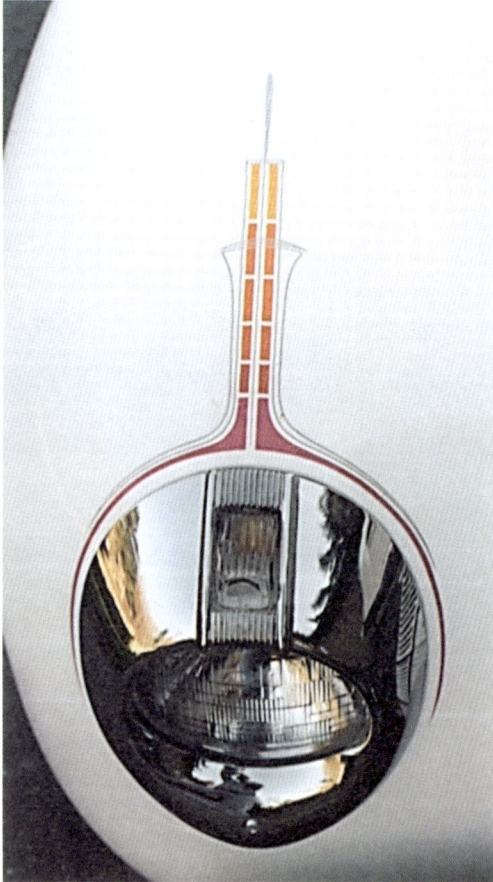

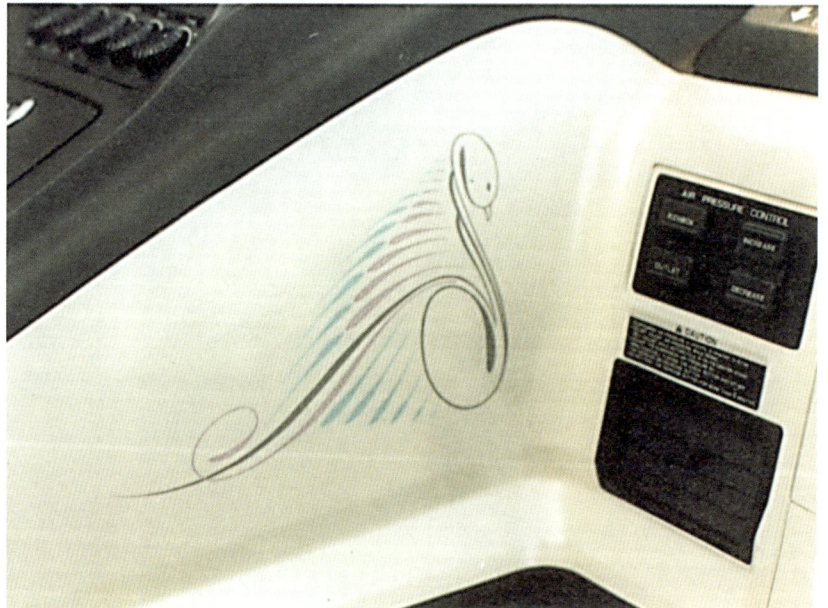

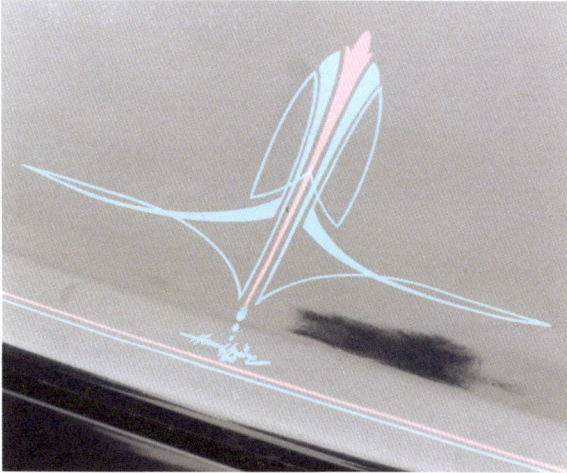

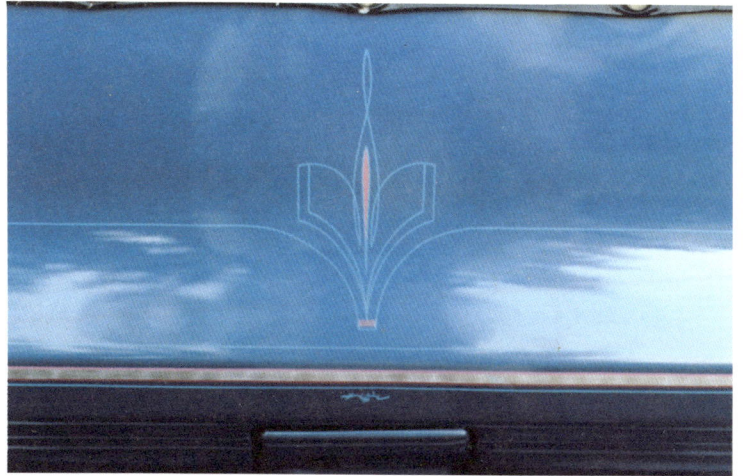

TERRY'S
APR
Washington
91
4T8MERC
48 MERC

John Hannukaine

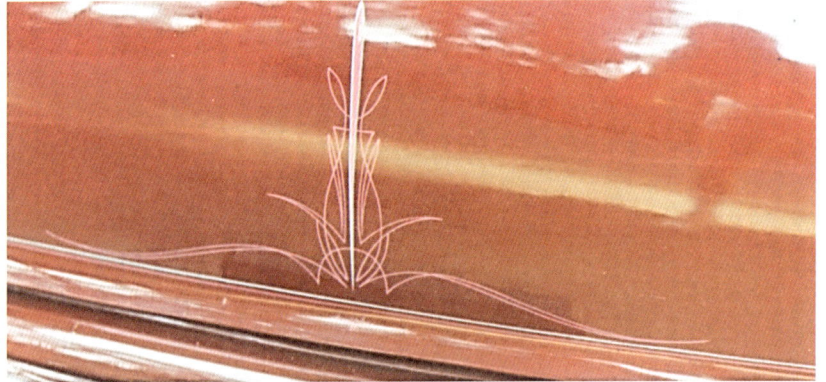

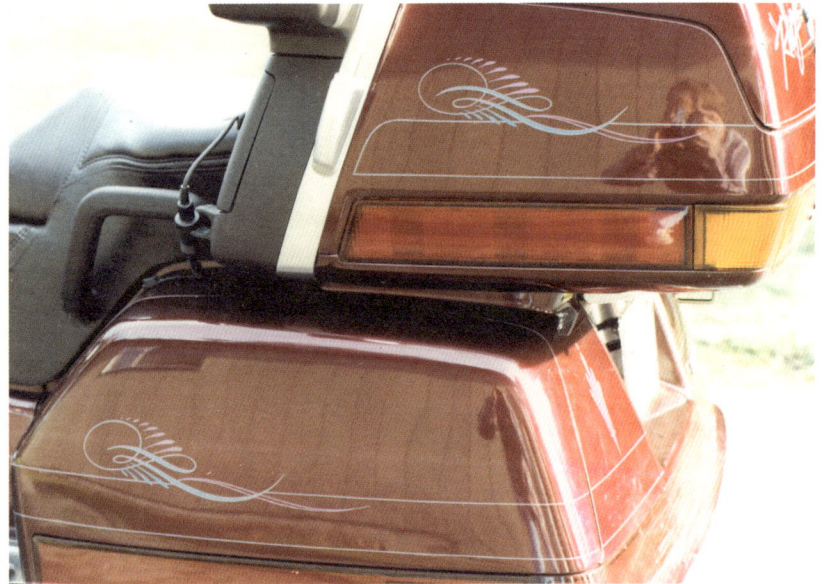

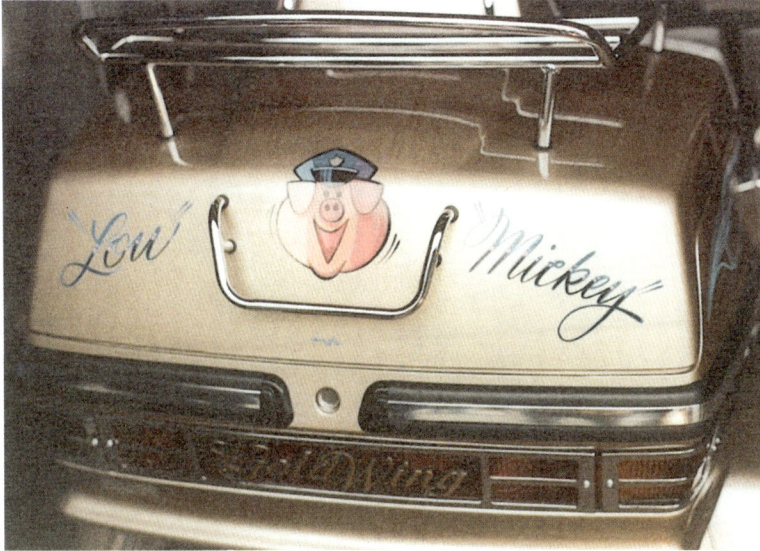
Cartoon, see page 83

Rose, see page 85

Pictorial, see page 91

Splatter effect, see page 69

Dry brush effect, see page 74

Sponge effect, see page 76

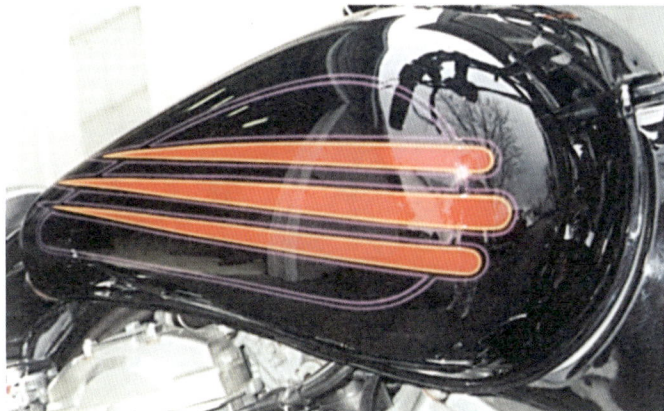

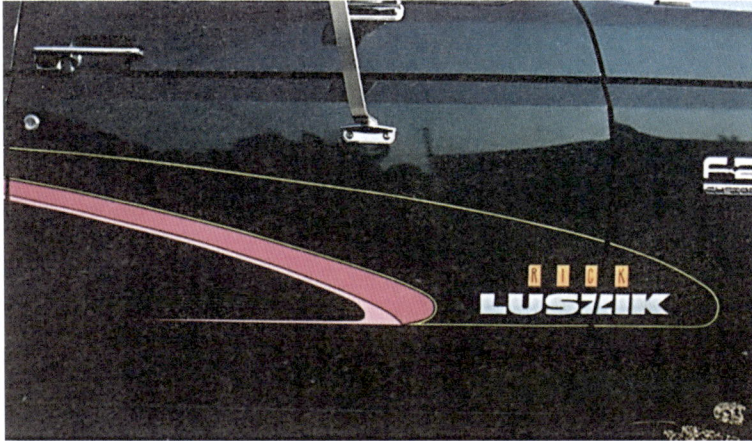

RICK
LUSZIK

Paradise
LANDSCAPES
756·3824

COWBOYS
XS·59BX

TOYOTA

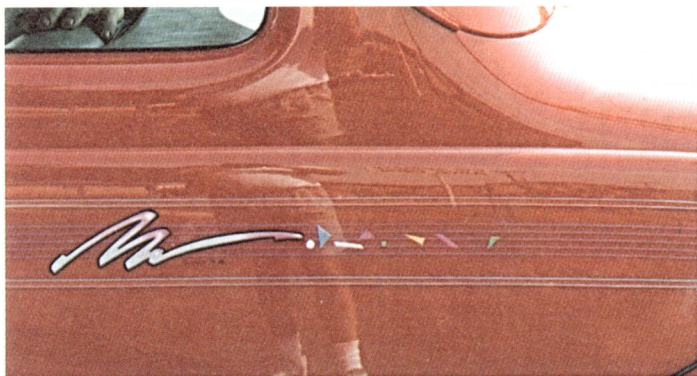

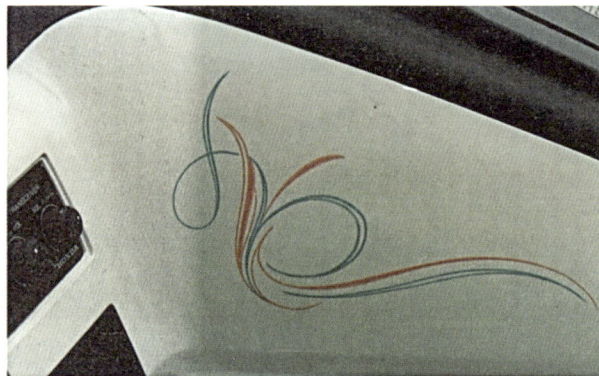

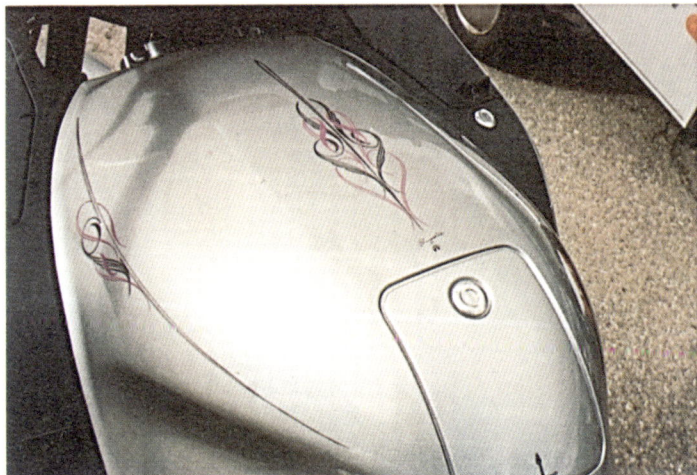

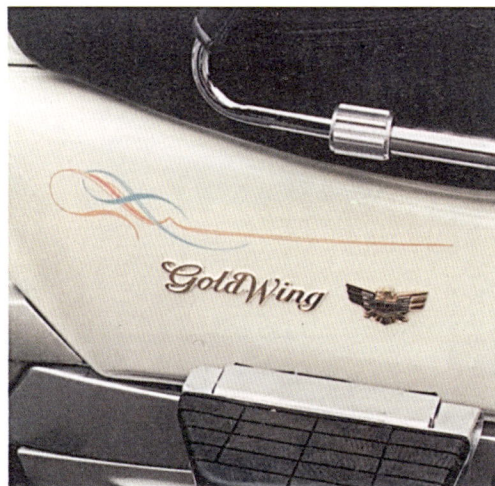

Jeff Stedje, *Wilderness Signs, St. Michael, Minnesota*   David Hightower, *Lawrence, Kansas*

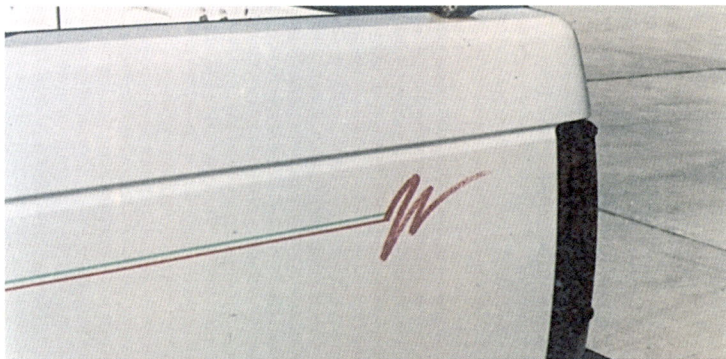

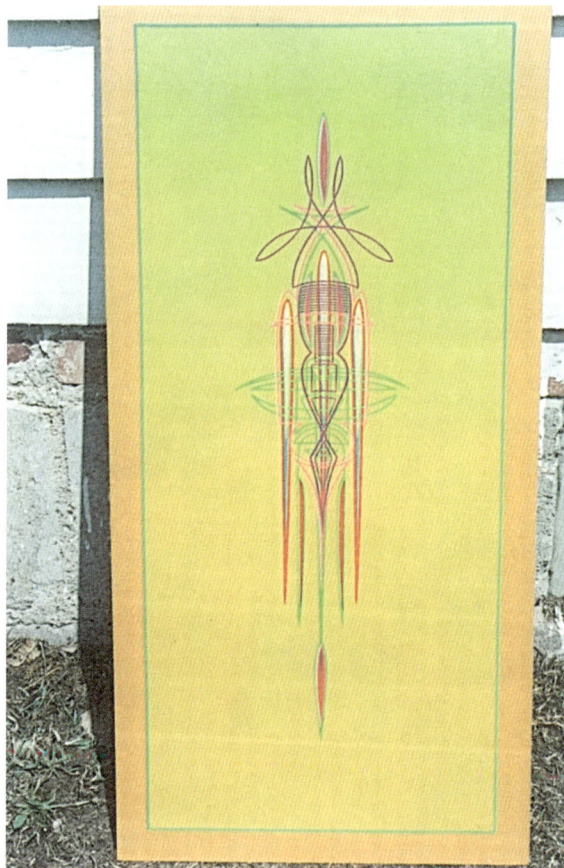

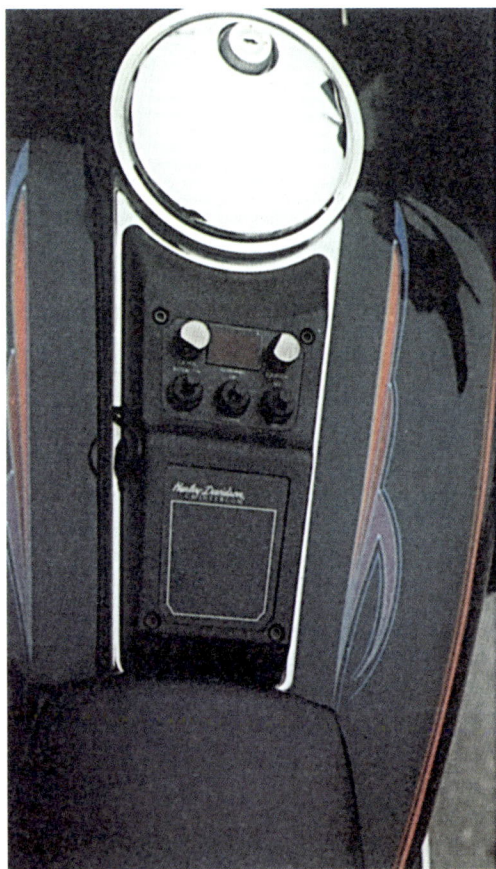

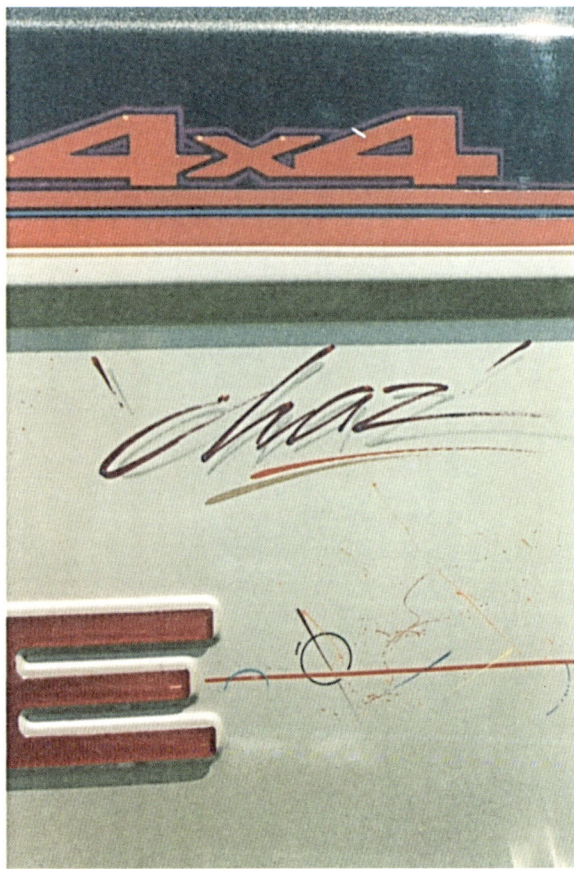

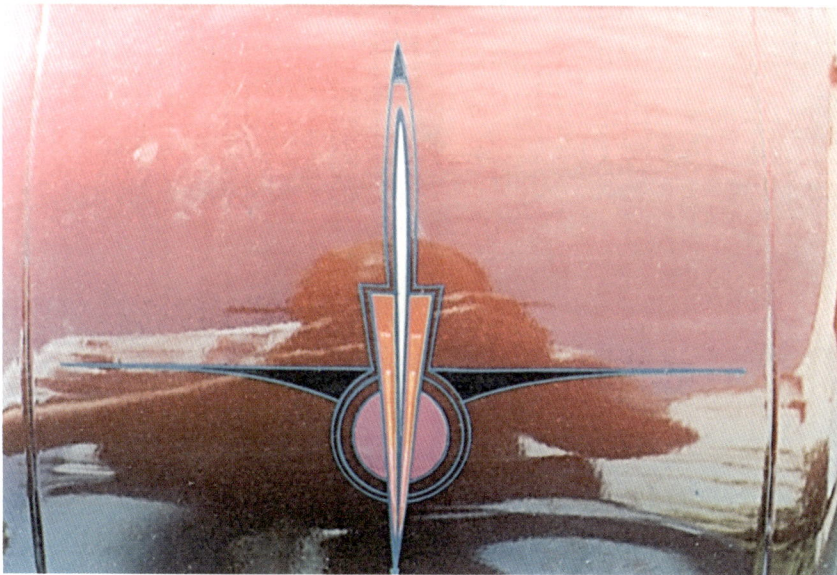

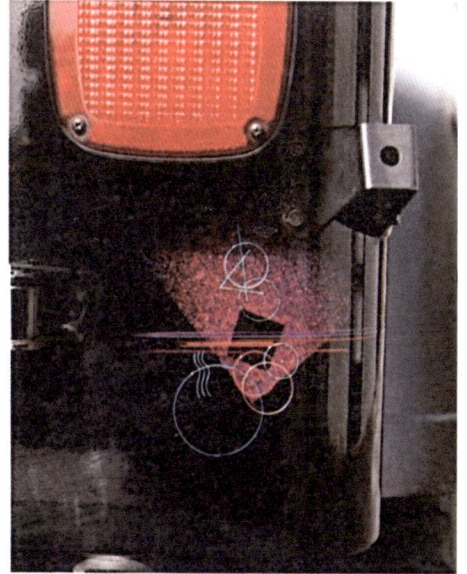

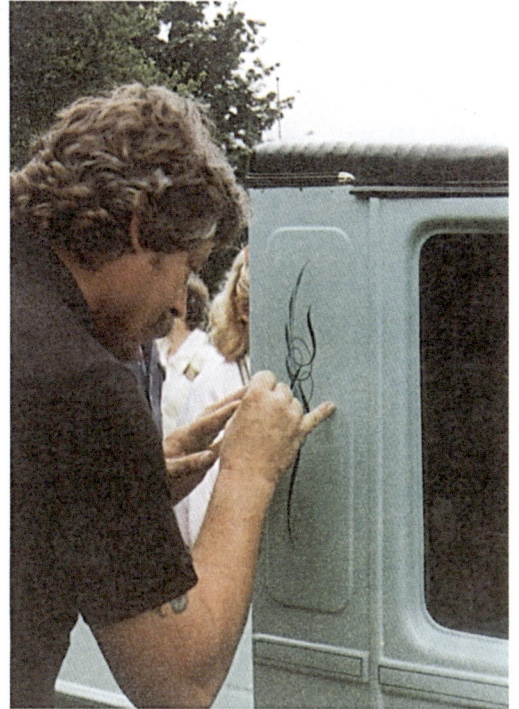

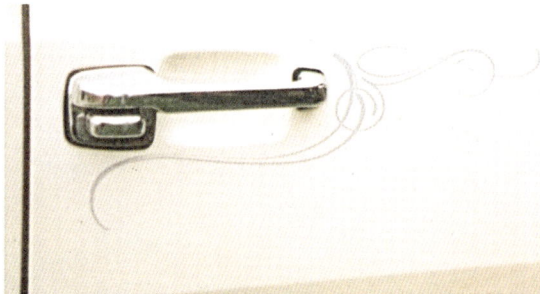

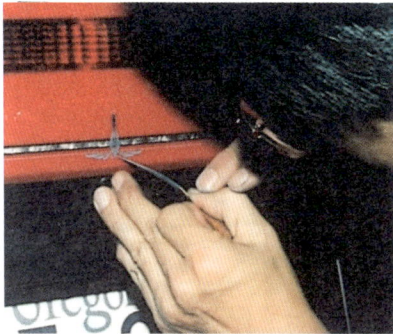

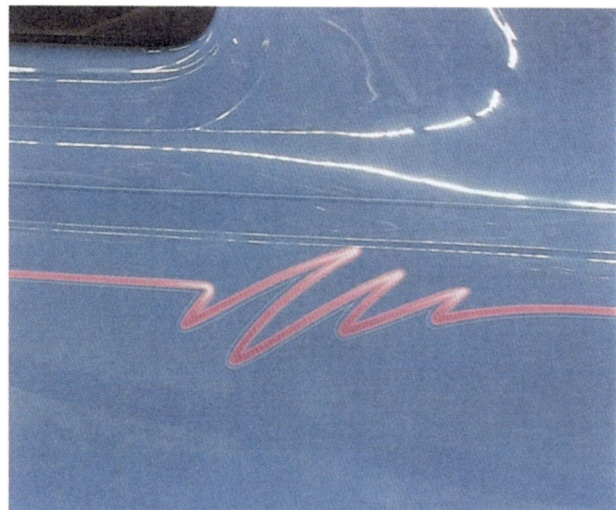

CHAPTER SEVEN: TIPS

Over the years, I have come across a few time-saving tips that make this work easier. Some I figured out on my own, others I learned from various stripers. Here are some of my favorites.

✗ I usually use the highest contrast color for the dominant part of the design.

✗ You'll be better off if you can paint a variety of styles. Different people like different things, and the variety will make your job much more interesting. Always be watching for new design and color ideas.

✗ Imitation gold: Mix "1 Shot" Bright Red, Lemon Yellow, and Imitation Silver in different proportions for variations in color. For paler shades, tint with ivory.

✗ I have a little sketch pad that I jot design ideas down in. It comes in handy when I run into a creativity "dry spell."

✗ Squinting at your work allows you to get an idea of what it will look like when seen from a reasonable viewing distance. Beware! It's extremely habit forming and people watching you stripe will think you're going blind.

✗ When necessary, I use an overcoat clear made by Martin Senour Co. It's called 8040 Clear, and is available from Martin Senour Co., 101 Prospect Ave., Cleveland, OH 44115.

✗ After the paint is dry, I usually take a water-dampened cloth or paper towel and wipe over the painted area. This will remove any Stabilo lines or powder that I use on my hands.

✗ If you hit a design you like while practicing, lay a piece of paper over the wet paint, squeegee with a vinyl squeegee, and it will transfer to the paper.

✗ Use an inexpensive compass for laying out guidelines around wheel wells, etc. Cover the sharp point with masking tape, and put a Stabilo pencil in the holder.

✗ Here are some great sources for design and color ideas:
Grocery stores — when I'm trying to design a logo, or if I need some help with colors, I'll walk the aisles, soaking up all the shapes and colors. It usually does the job.
Car magazines
Clothing stores
And, of course, *SignCraft* Magazine!

✗ Another gold formula: For a wonderful striping and lettering gold, mix Cres-Lite Superfine Bronze Powder (available in many colors) with Royal Gard Spar Varnish. This product is designed for interior use, but it works on bikes and show vehicles, because they usually live inside. For exterior use, I use

Cres-Lite Resisto Powder. It's not ground as fine as the Superfine Powder, but it still works. The Cres-Lite powders are available from Crescent Bronze Powder Co., Inc., 1841 S. Flower St., Los Angeles, CA 90015. Royal Gard Spar Varnish is available through Dick Blick, P.O. Box 521, Henderson, NV 89015.

✗ Maintaining hand-painted vehicle graphics: Tell your customers to allow the paint to dry for three or four days before washing it. Lightly apply a coat of non-abrasive wax. Wash and wax it again a day or two later, then wash and wax the vehicle as you normally would. Rubbing compound, buffers, pressure washers, and automatic car washes should be avoided — they remove hand-painted graphics.

✗ To fix smudges made while pinstriping, wrap a rag around the pointed end of a striping brush, and clean off the smudge with a little denatured alcohol.

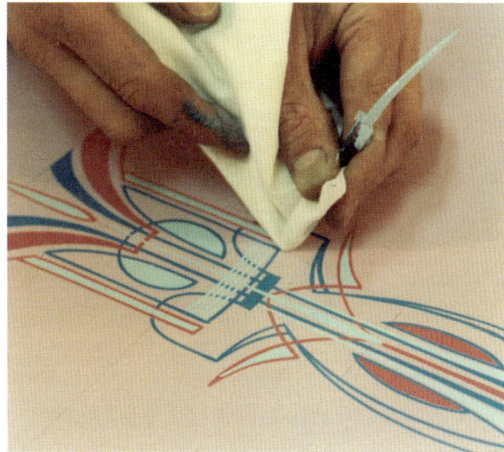

To learn more about pinstriping,
vehicle graphics, sign making
and lettering, subscribe to
SignCraft Magazine, P.O.Box 60031,
Fort Myers, Florida 33906
239-939-4644
800-204-0204
www.signcraft.com